TIMELESS PRAISE

CONTENTS

– PIANO LEVEL –
EARLY INTERMEDIATE
(HLSPL LEVEL 4-5)

ISBN 978-0-634-02583-9

HAL•LEONARD®
CORPORATION
7777 W. BLUEMOUND RD. P.O. BOX 13819 MILWAUKEE, WI 53213

Visit Hal Leonard Online at
www.halleonard.com

PREFACE

Many beautiful praise songs have been written in recent years. Some of these will last beyond contemporary popularity and bring their timeless messages to new generations. Something in their magical combination of poignant melody and lyric will continue to inspire worshiping people, even when musical styles have moved into new sonic terrain.

Although these songs have been arranged for piano, allow the lyrics to inform your instrumental interpretation. If you memorize the music for a performance, take the lyric to heart as well. It will bring further depth to your melodic phrasing.

As one timeless song from another century says:

> *"When we've been there ten thousand years,*
> *Bright shining as the sun,*
> *We've no less days to sing God's praise*
> *Than when we'd first begun."*

("Amazing Grace" 5th stanza by John P. Rees)

Sincerely,
Phillip Keveren

◆

BIOGRAPHY

Phillip Keveren, a multi-talented keyboard artist and composer, has composed original works in a variety of genres from piano solo to symphonic orchestra. Mr. Keveren gives frequent concerts and workshops for teachers and their students in the United States, Canada, Europe, and Asia. Mr. Keveren holds a B.M. in composition from California State University Northridge and a M.M. in composition from the University of Southern California.

GREAT IS THE LORD

Words and Music by MICHAEL W. SMITH
and DEBORAH D. SMITH

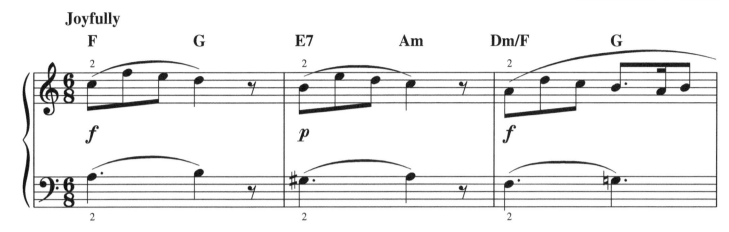

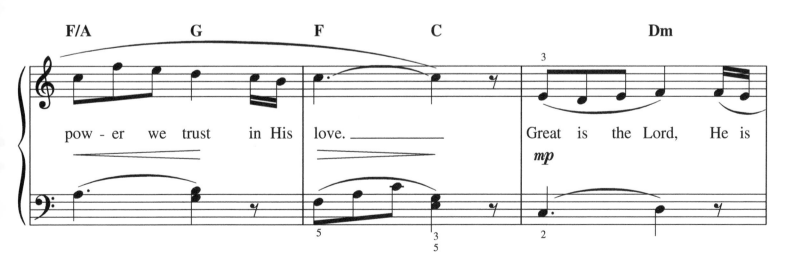

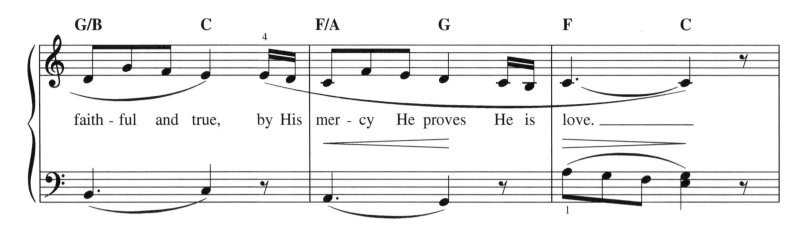

faith - ful and true, by His mer - cy He proves He is love. _____

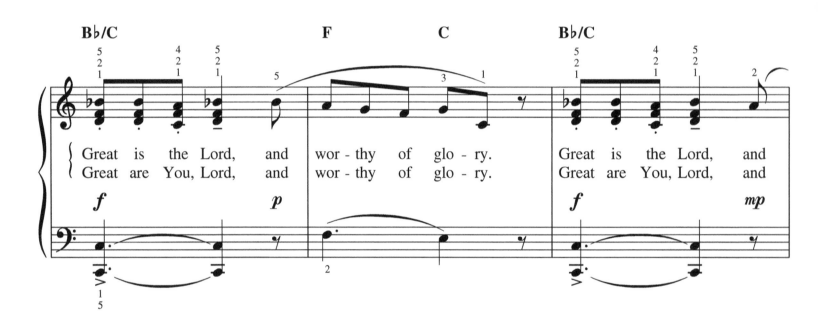

Great is the Lord, and wor - thy of glo - ry.
Great are You, Lord, and wor - thy of glo - ry.

Great is the Lord, and
Great are You, Lord, and

wor - thy of praise.
wor - thy of praise.

Great is the Lord, now
Great are You, Lord, I

lift up your voice, Now
lift up my voice, I

lift up your voice:
lift up my voice:
Great
Great
is the
are You,
Lord!
Lord!

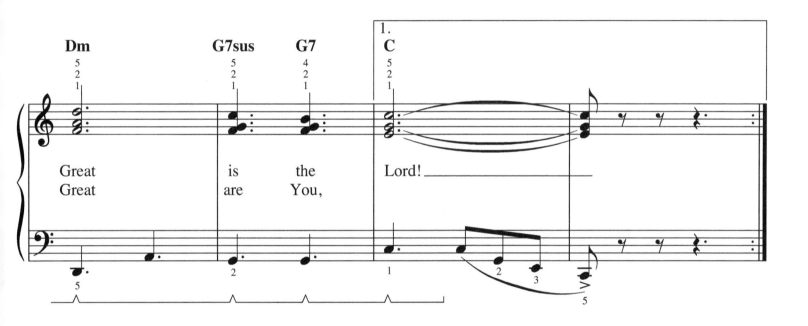

Great
Great
is the
are You,
Lord!

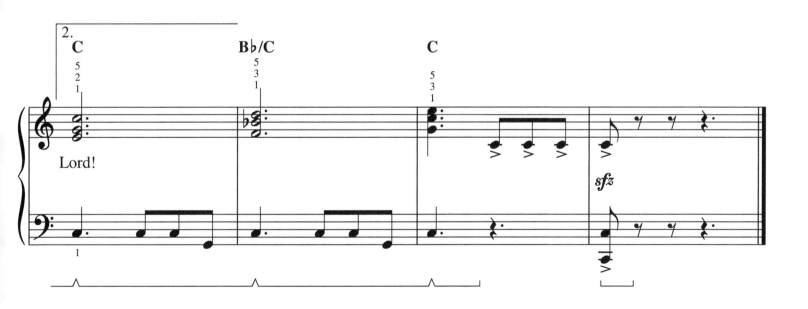

Lord!

AS THE DEER

Words and Music by
MARTIN NYSTROM

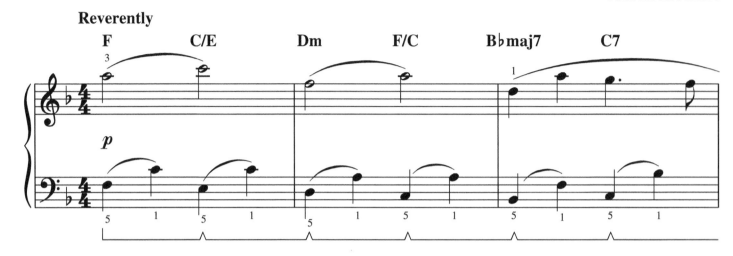

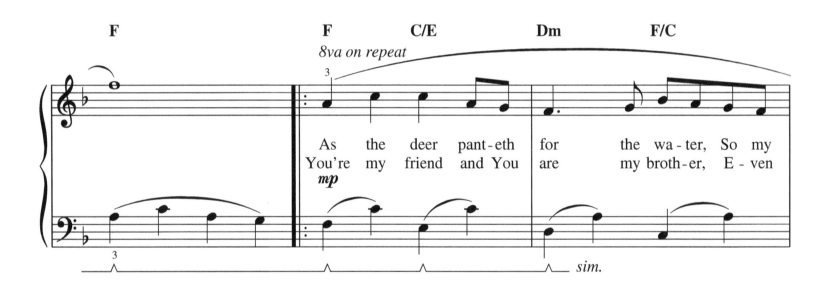

As the deer pant-eth for the wa-ter, So my
You're my friend and You are my broth-er, E-ven

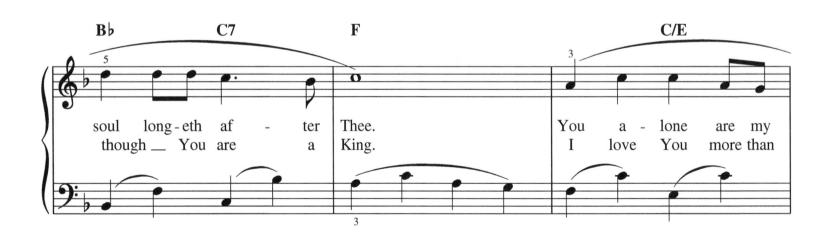

soul long-eth af-ter Thee.
though __ You are a King.

You a-lone are my
I love You more than

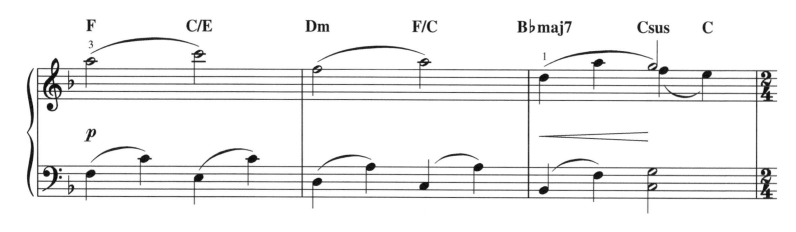

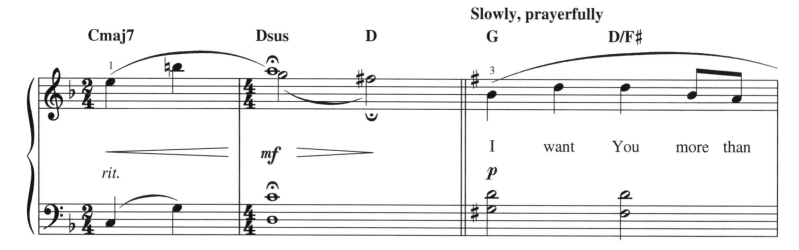

I want You more than

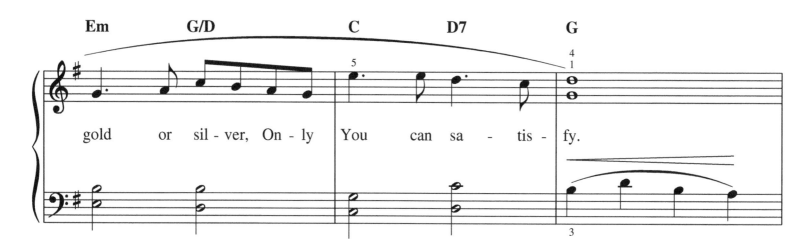

gold or sil - ver, On - ly You can sa - tis - fy.

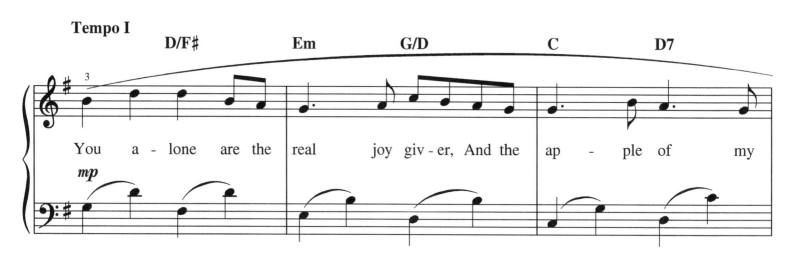

You a - lone are the real joy giv - er, And the ap - ple of my

DID YOU FEEL THE MOUNTAINS TREMBLE?

Words and Music by
MARTIN SMITH

EL SHADDAI

Words and Music by MICHAEL CARD
and JOHN THOMPSON

With deep reverence

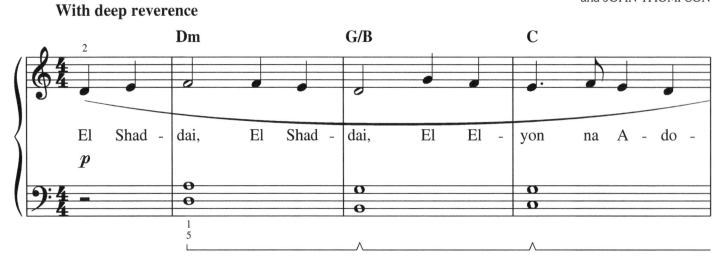

El Shad - dai, El Shad - dai, El El - yon na A - do -

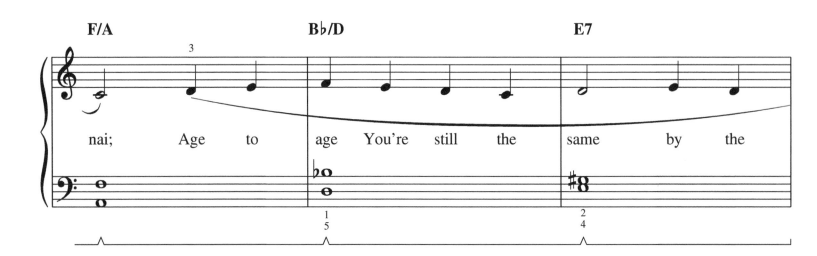

nai; Age to age You're still the same by the

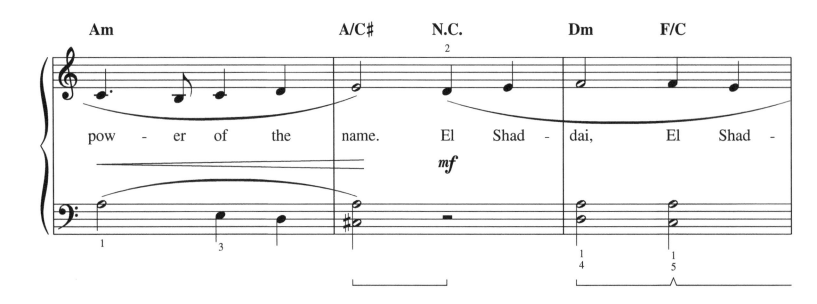

pow - er of the name. El Shad - dai, El Shad -

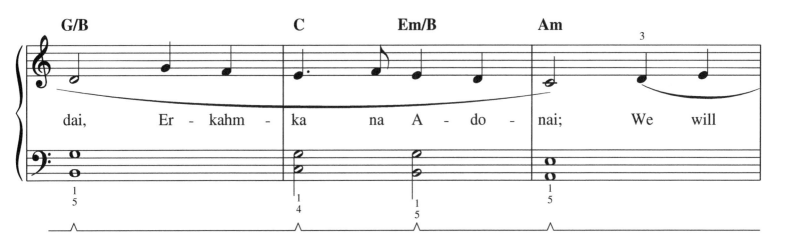

dai,   Er - kahm - ka   na   A - do - nai;   We   will

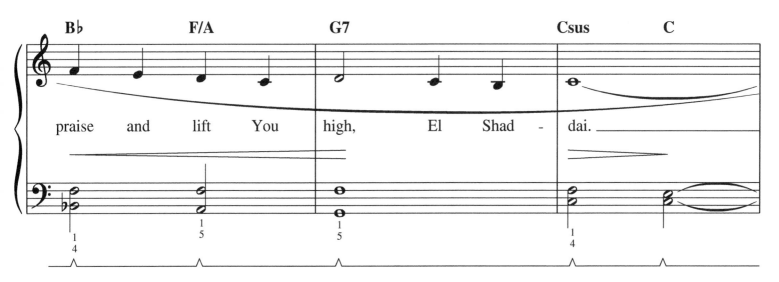

praise   and   lift   You   high,   El   Shad - dai. _____

Variation 1:

With motion

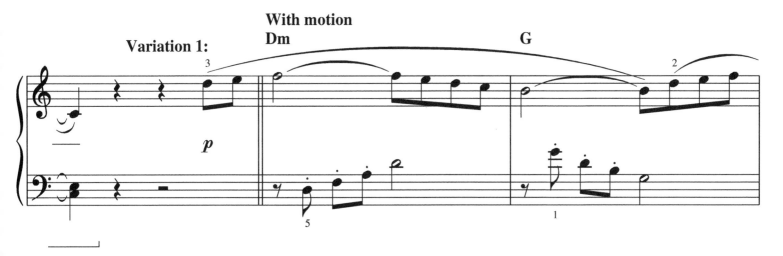

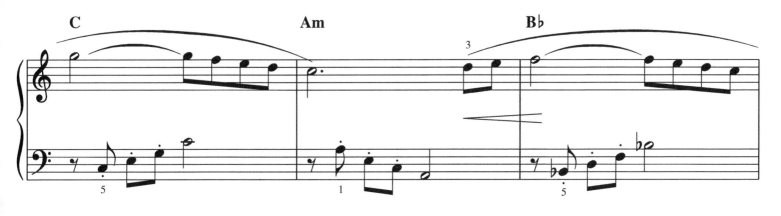

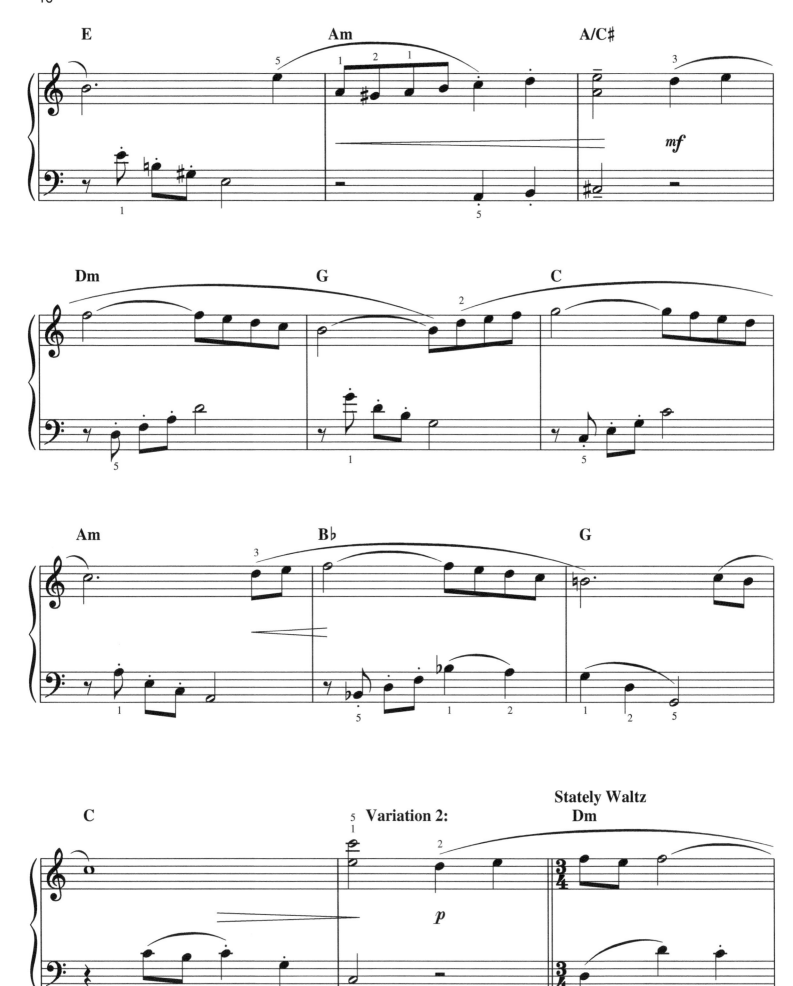

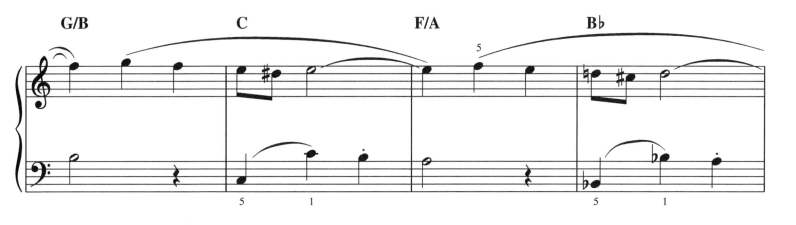

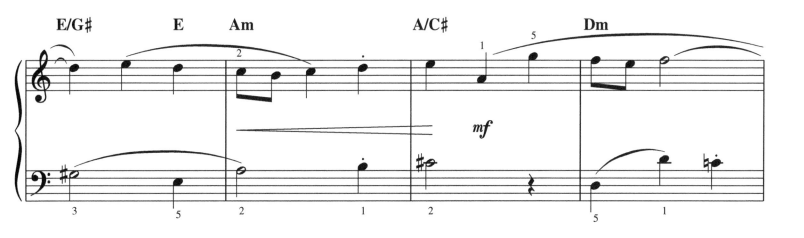

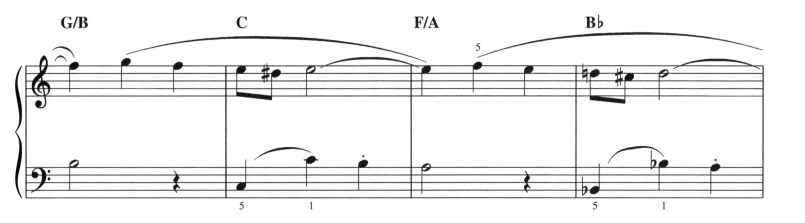

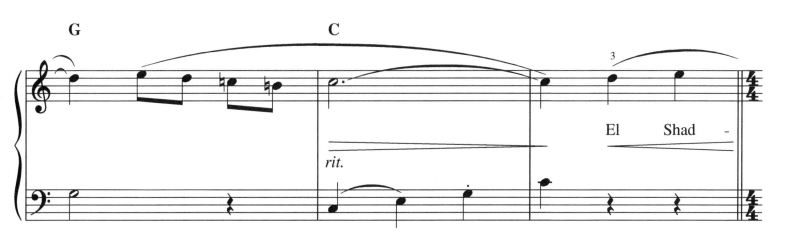

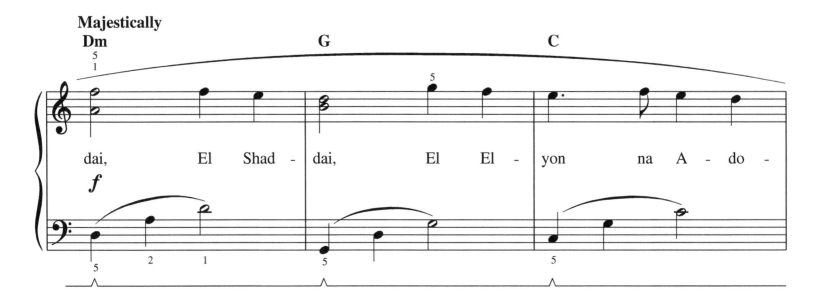

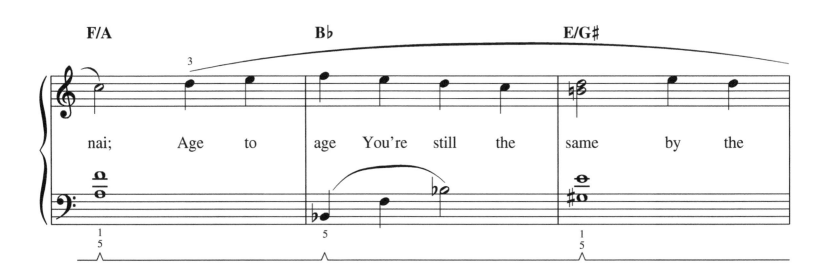

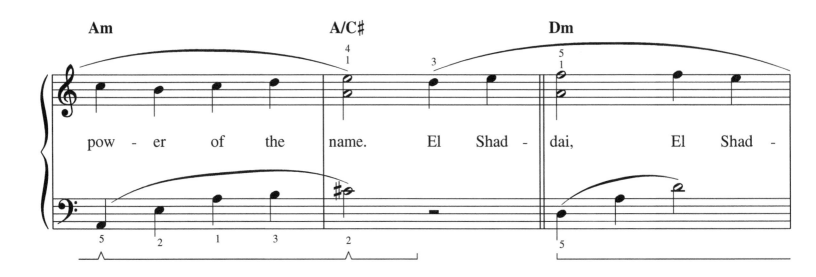

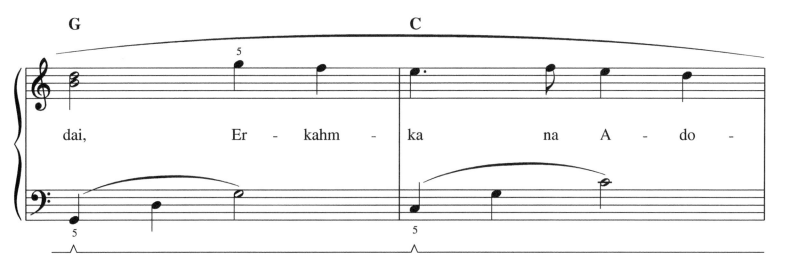

dai, Er - kahm - ka na A - do -

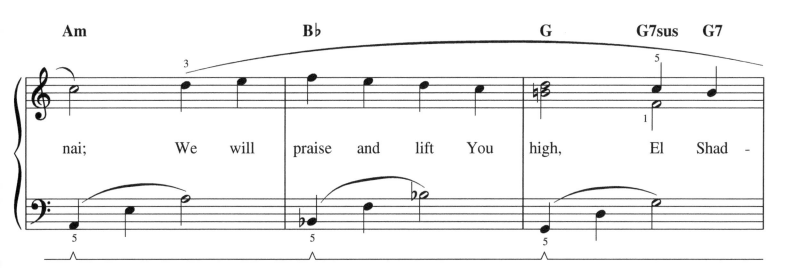

nai; We will praise and lift You high, El Shad -

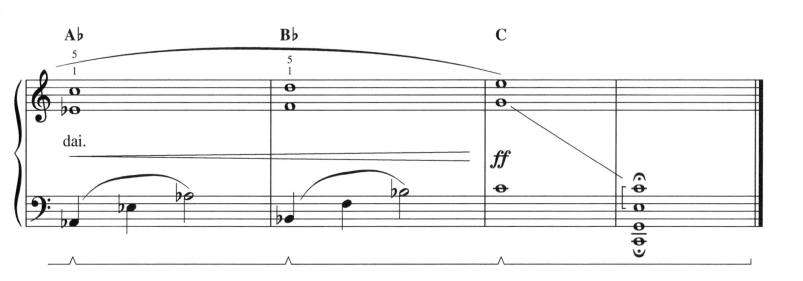

dai.

GIVE THANKS

Words and Music by
HENRY SMITH

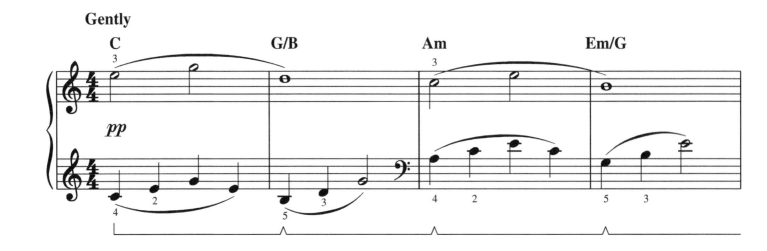

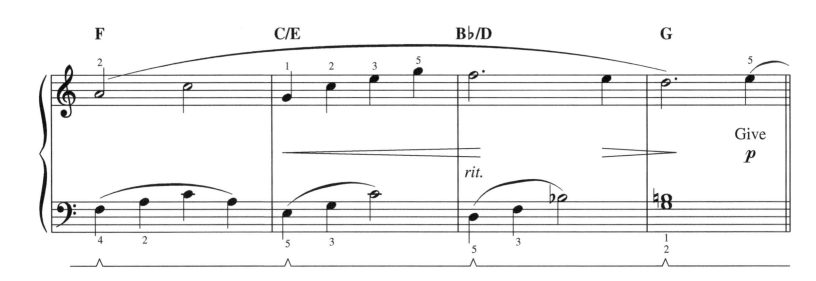

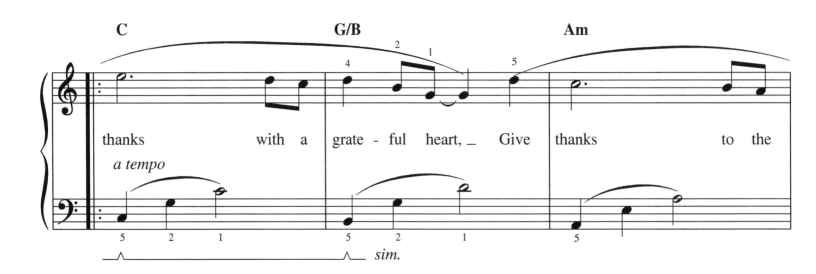

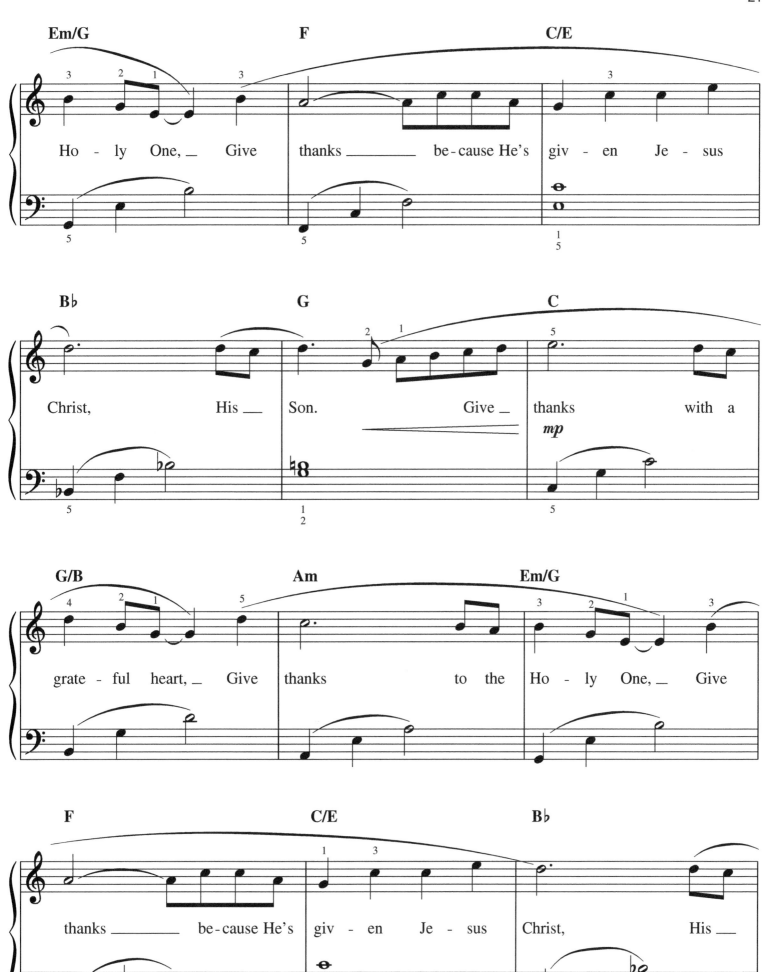

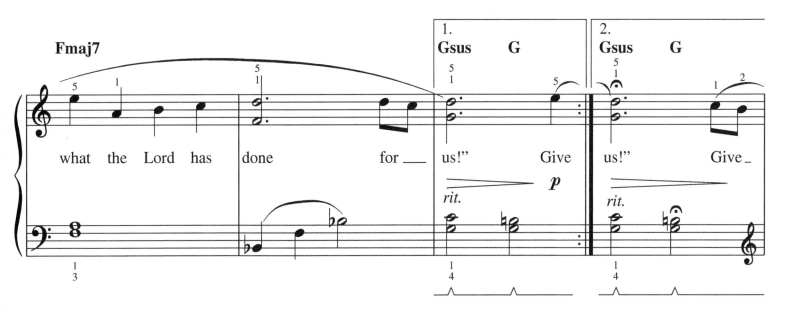

what the Lord has done for ___ us!" Give us!" Give

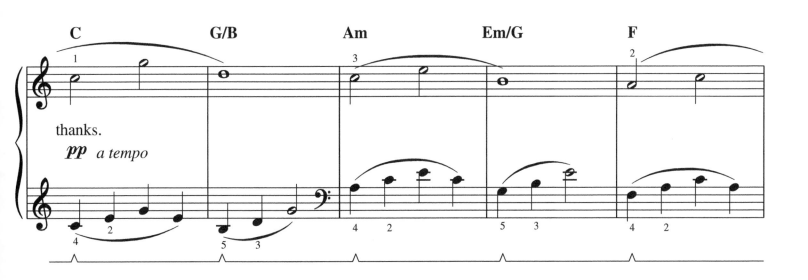

thanks.

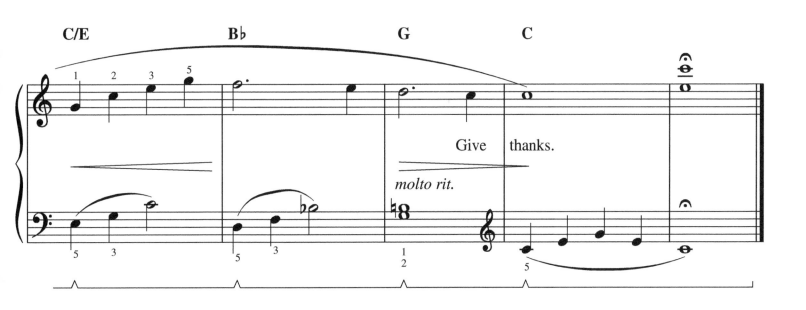

Give thanks.

HE IS EXALTED

Words and Music by
TWILA PARIS

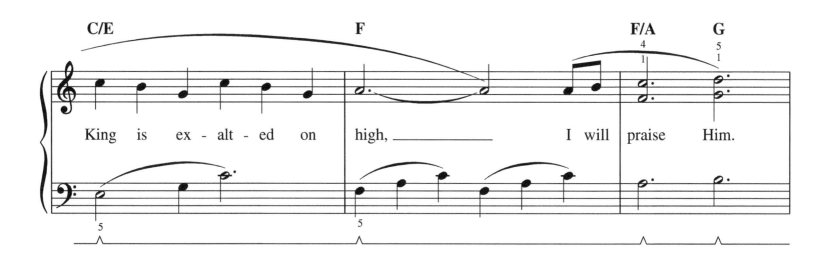

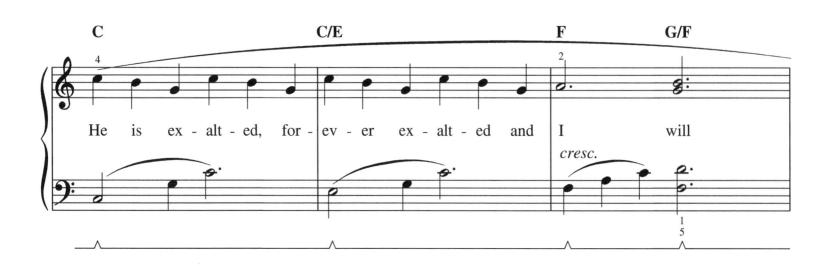

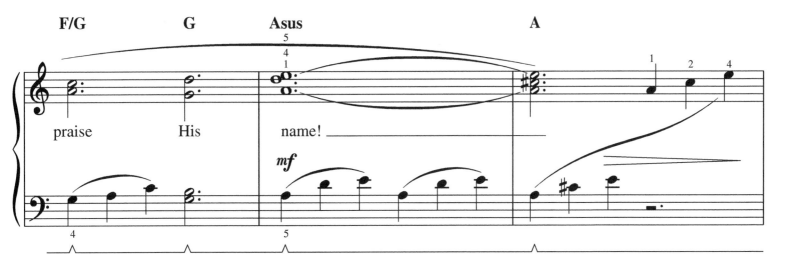

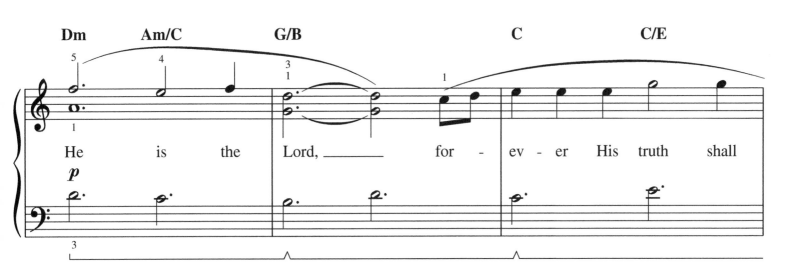

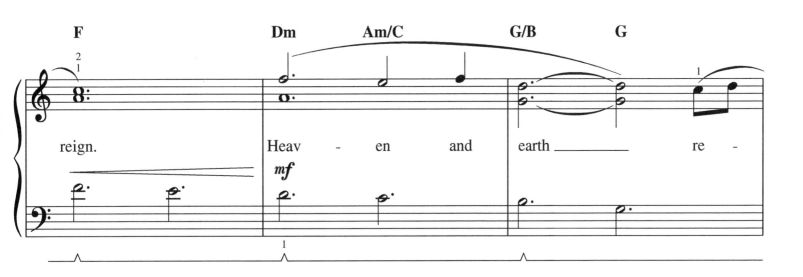

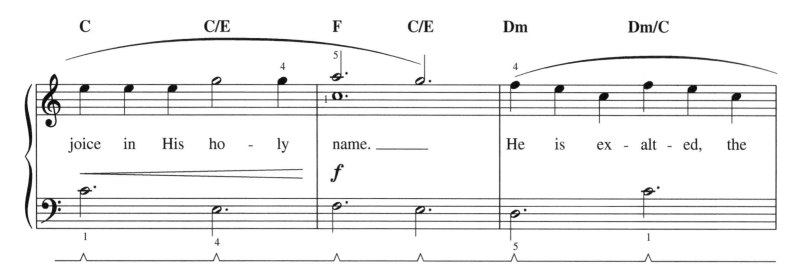

joice in His ho - ly name. _____ He is ex - alt - ed, the

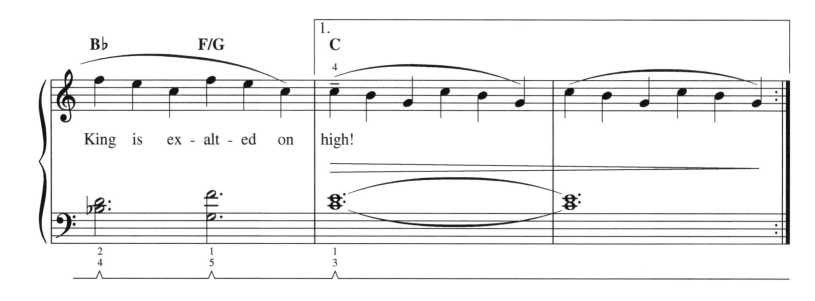

King is ex - alt - ed on high!

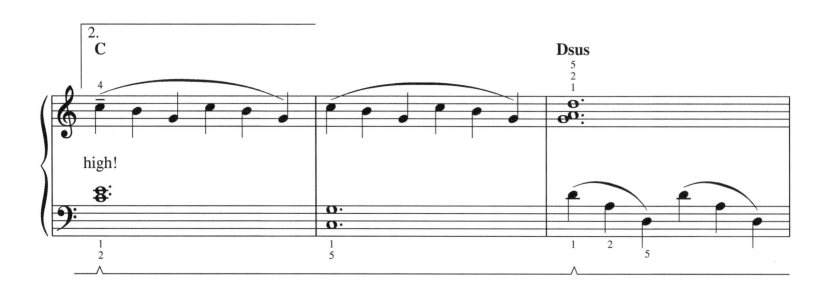

high!

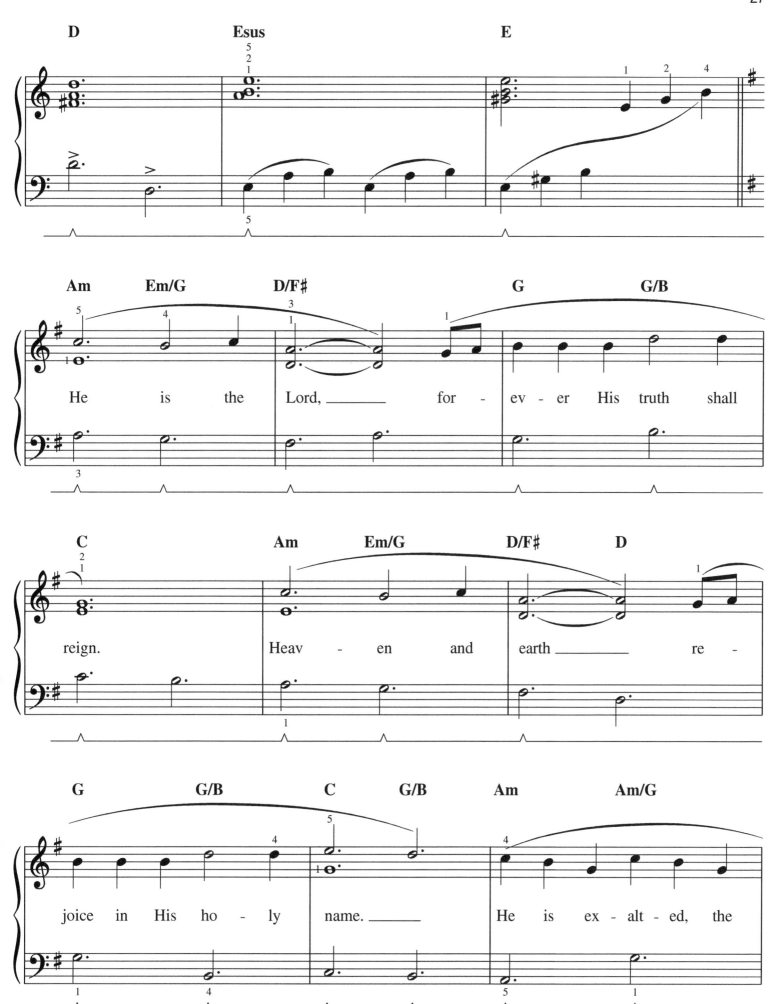

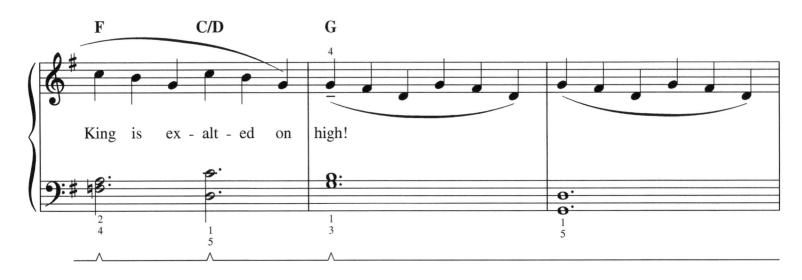

King is ex - alt - ed on high!

rit.

He is ex - alt - ed, the

ff

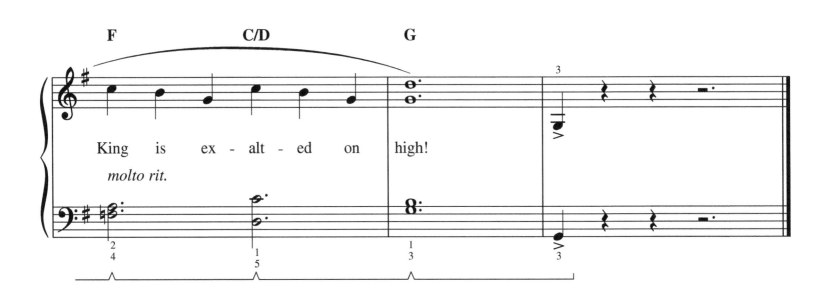

King is ex - alt - ed on high!

molto rit.

HOW BEAUTIFUL

Words and Music by
TWILA PARIS

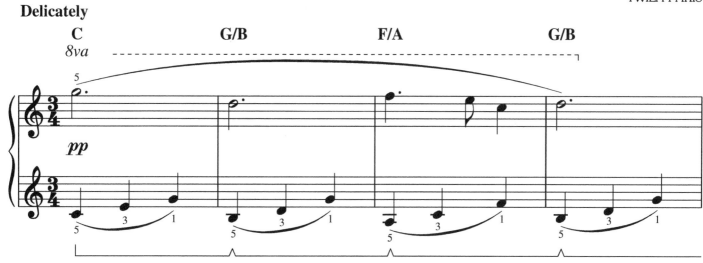

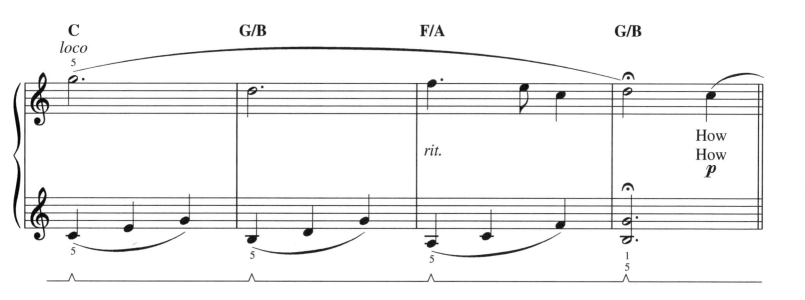

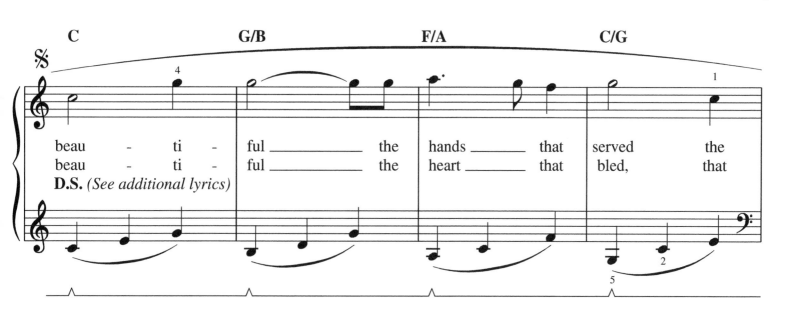

30

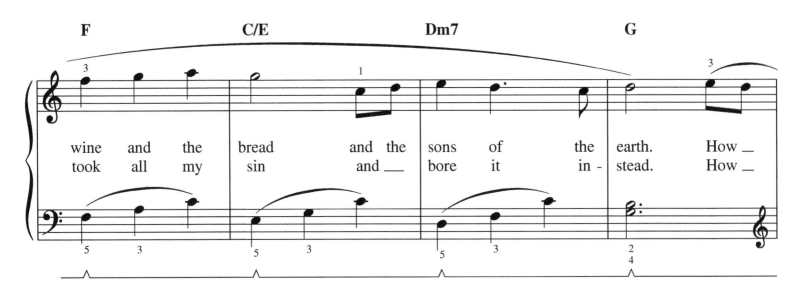

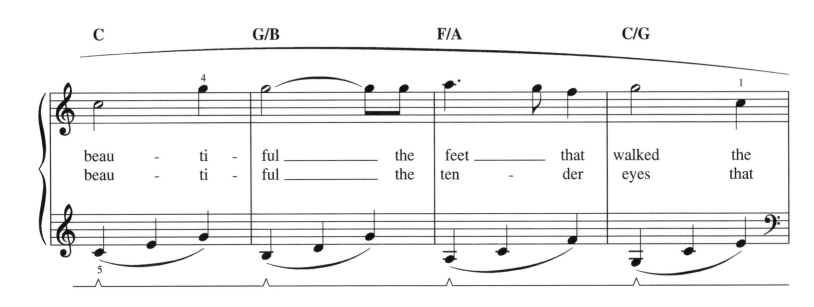

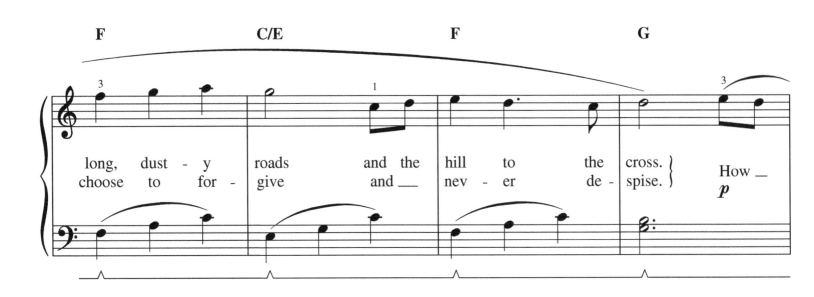

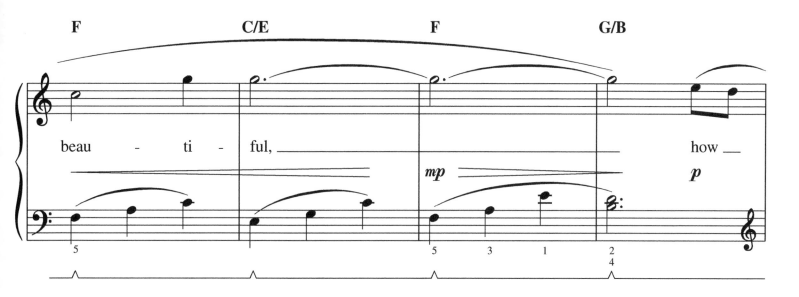

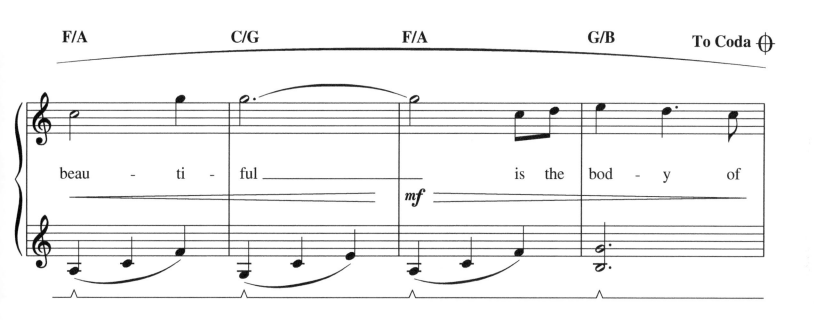

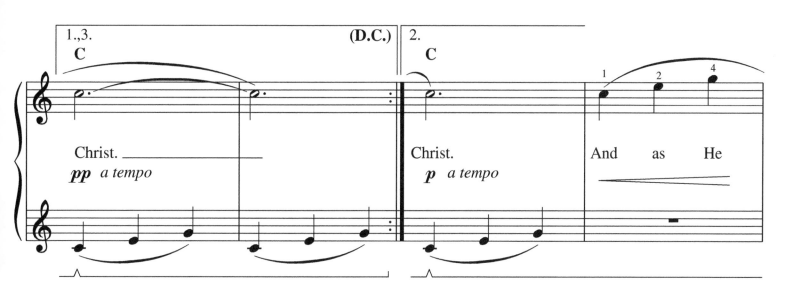

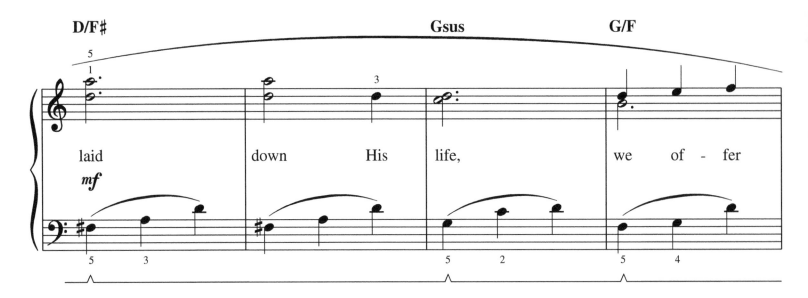

D/F♯   Gsus   G/F

laid   down His   life,   we of - fer

mf

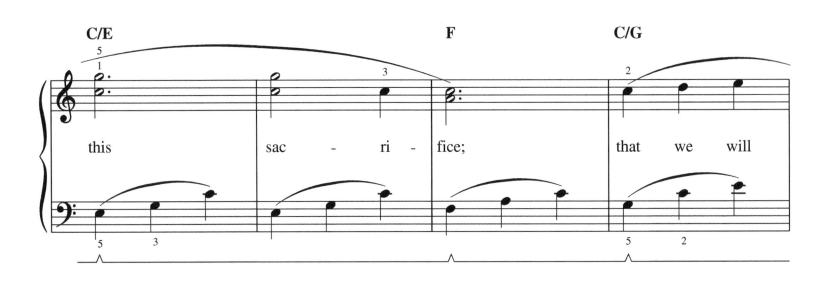

C/E   F   C/G

this   sac - ri - fice;   that we will

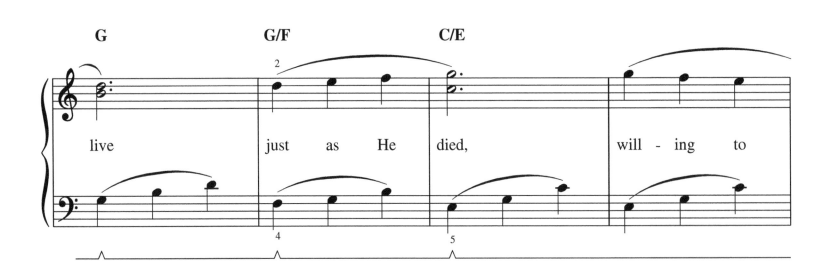

G   G/F   C/E

live   just as He died,   will - ing to

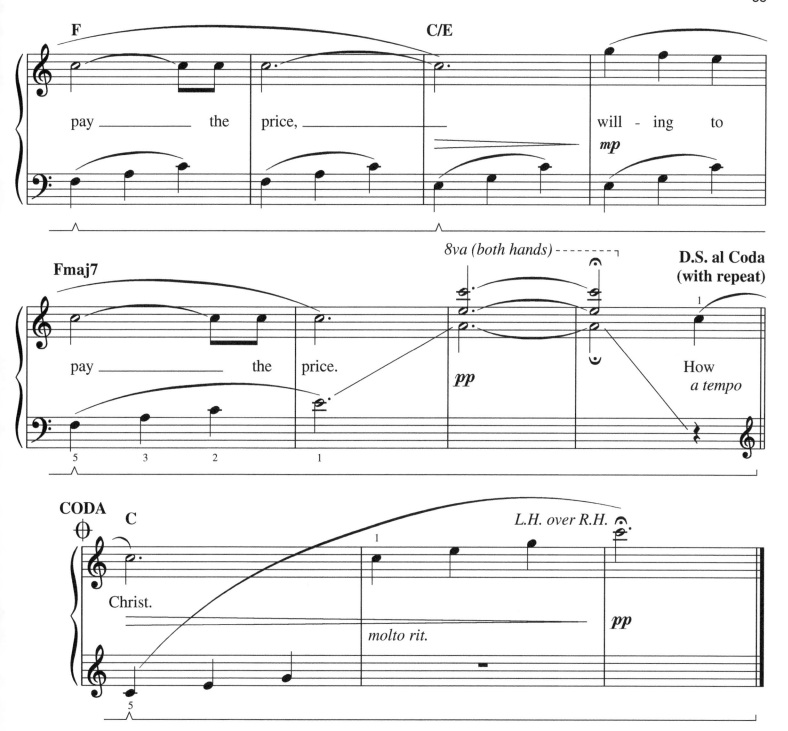

Additional Lyrics

3. How beautiful the radiant Bride
   Who waits for her Groom with His light in her eyes.
   How beautiful when humble hearts give
   The fruit of pure lives so that others may live.
   How beautiful, how beautiful,
   How beautiful is the body of Christ.

4. How beautiful the feet that bring
   The sound of good news and the love of the King.
   How beautiful the hands that serve
   The wine and the bread and the sons of the earth.
   How beautiful, how beautiful,
   How beautiful is the body of Christ.

HOW MAJESTIC IS YOUR NAME

Words and Music by
MICHAEL W. SMITH

With grandeur

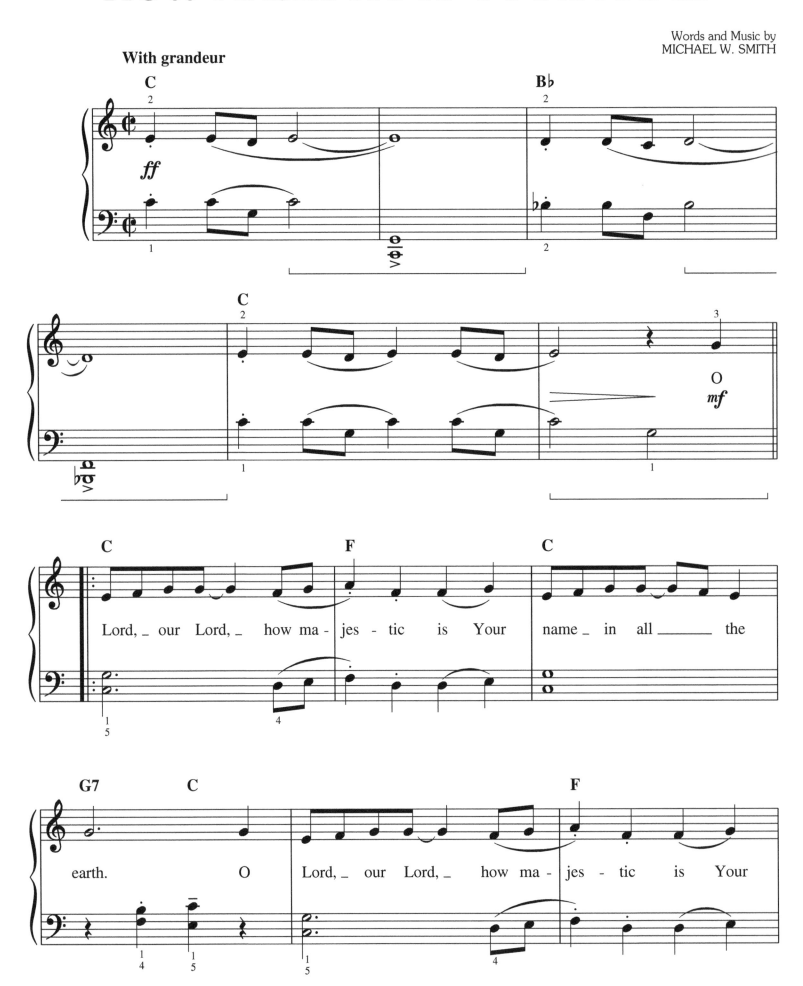

Lord, _ our Lord, _ how ma - jes - tic is Your name _ in all _____ the

earth.   O   Lord, _ our Lord, _ how ma - jes - tic is Your

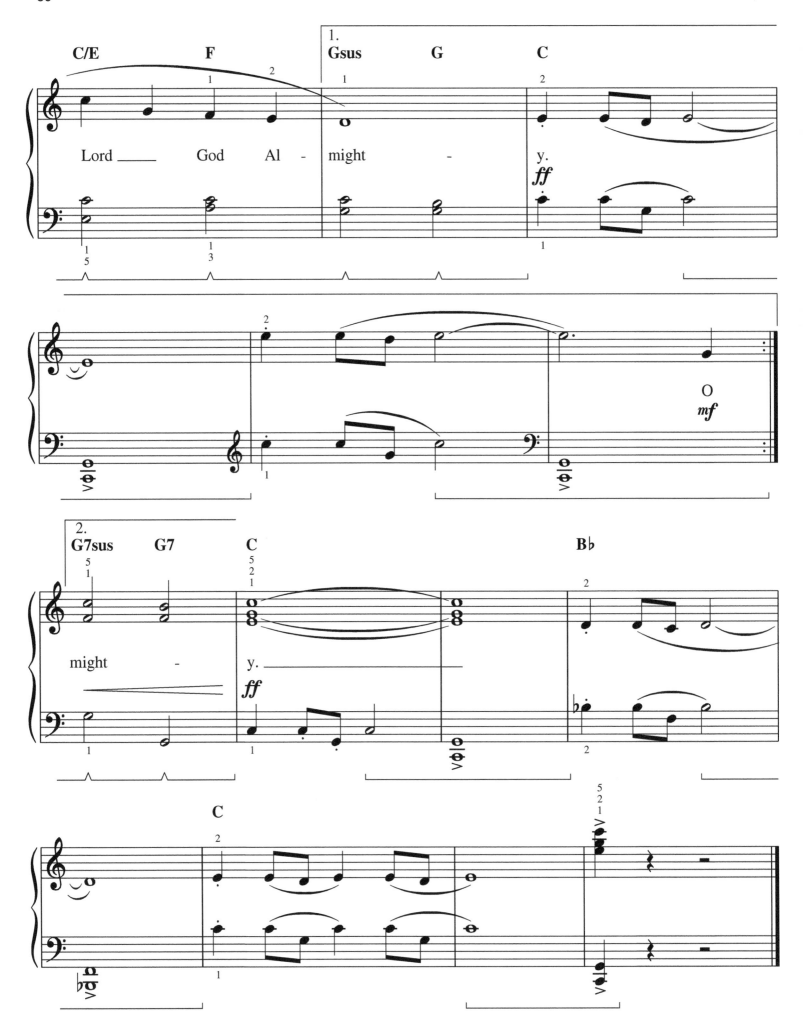

LORD, I LIFT YOUR NAME ON HIGH

Words and Music by
RICK FOUNDS

I COULD SING OF YOUR LOVE FOREVER

Words and Music by
MARTIN SMITH

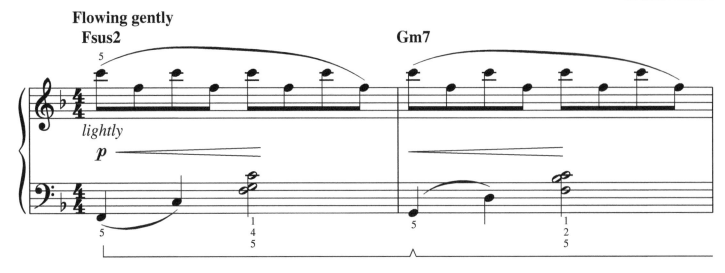

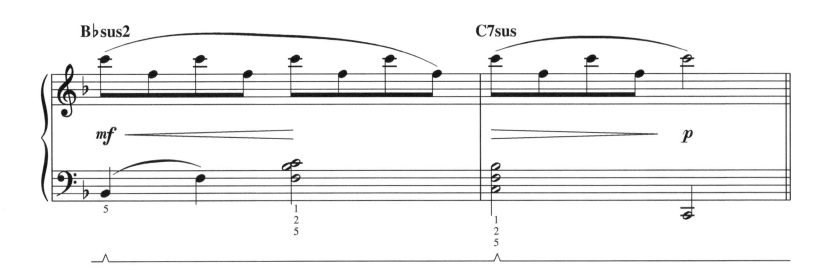

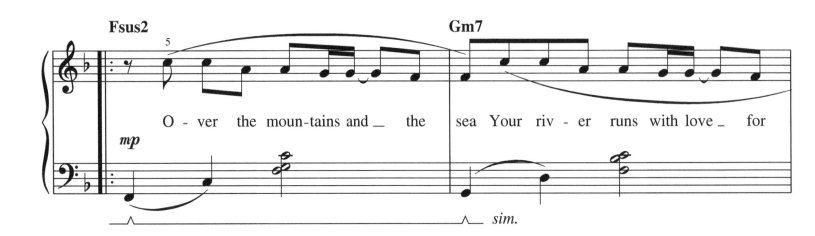

O - ver the moun-tains and __ the sea Your riv - er runs with love __ for

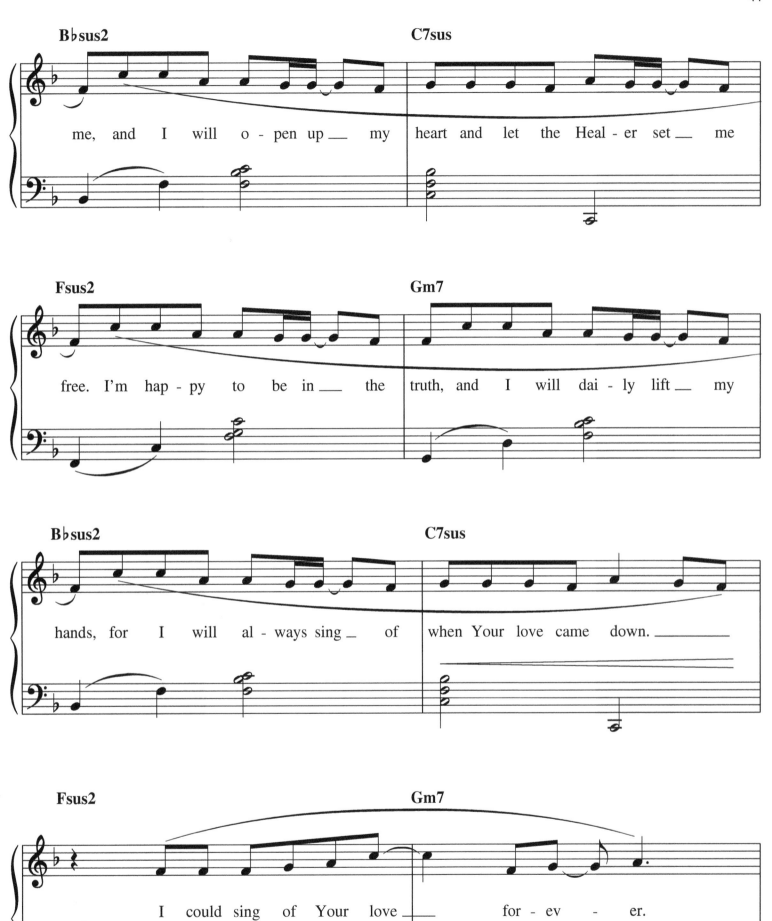

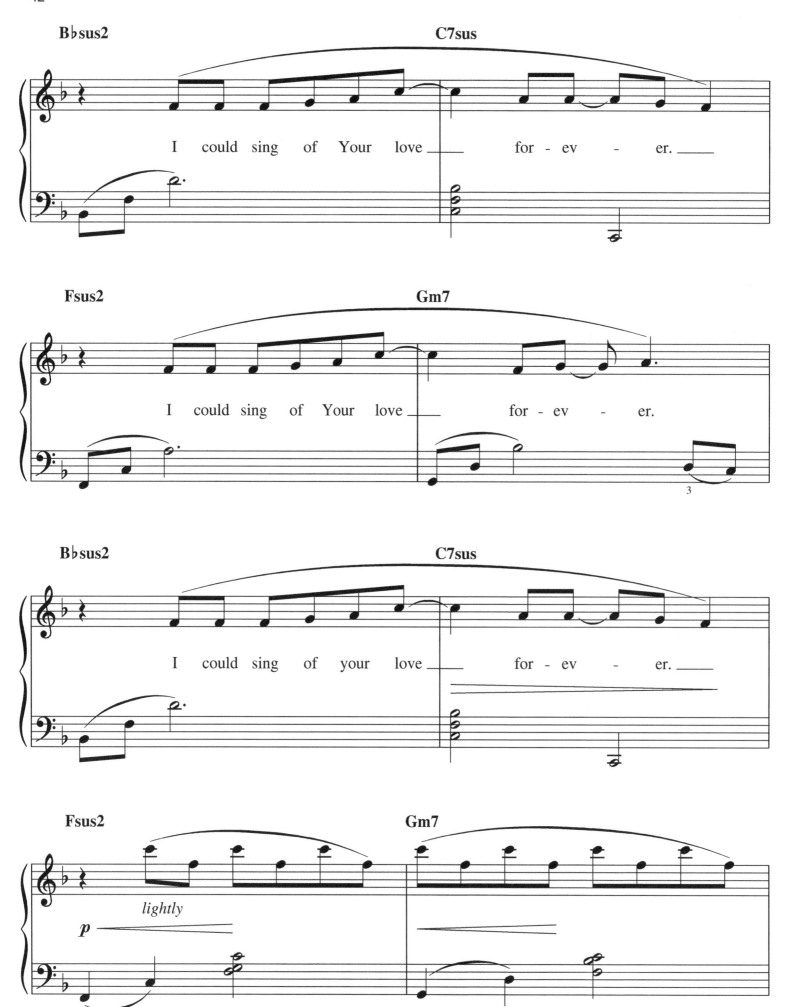

MORE PRECIOUS THAN SILVER

Words and Music by
LYNN DeSHAZO

Simply, with warmth

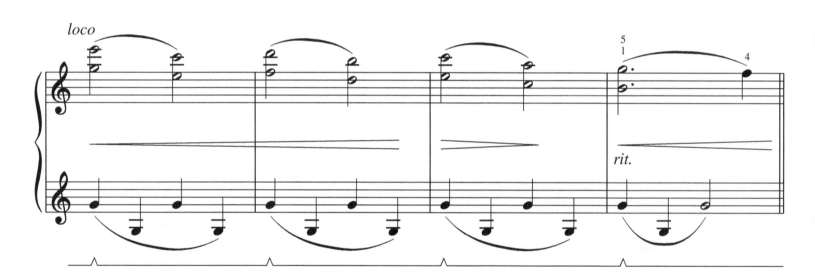

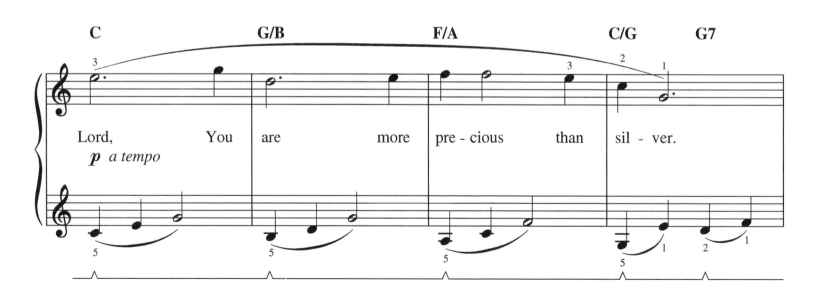

Lord, You are more pre - cious than sil - ver.

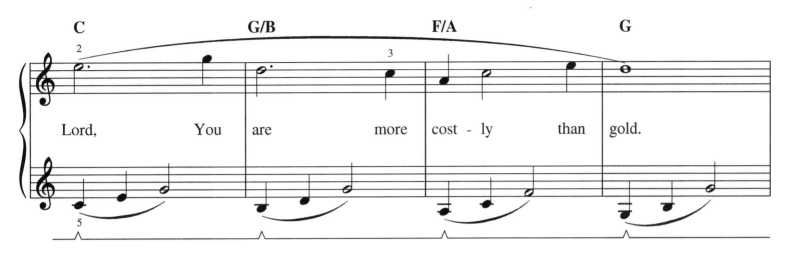

Lord, You are more cost - ly than gold.

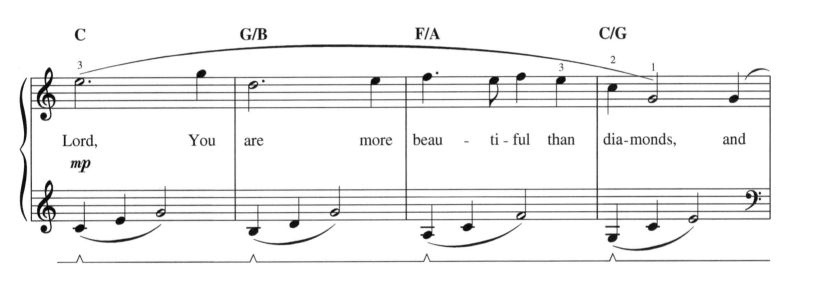

Lord, You are more beau - ti - ful than dia - monds, and

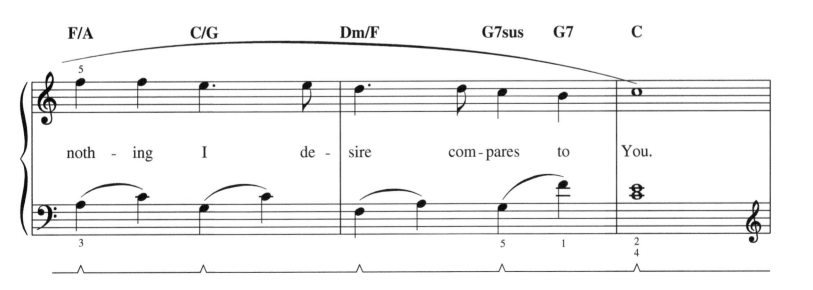

noth - ing I de - sire com - pares to You.

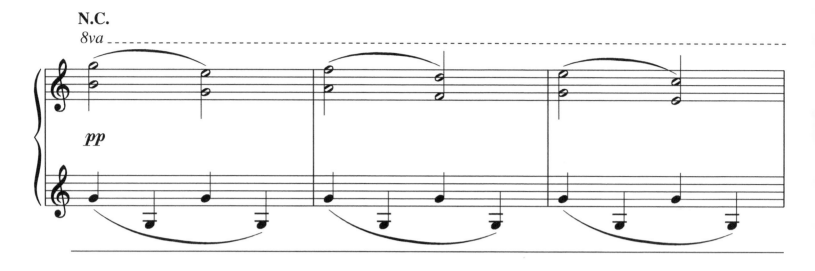

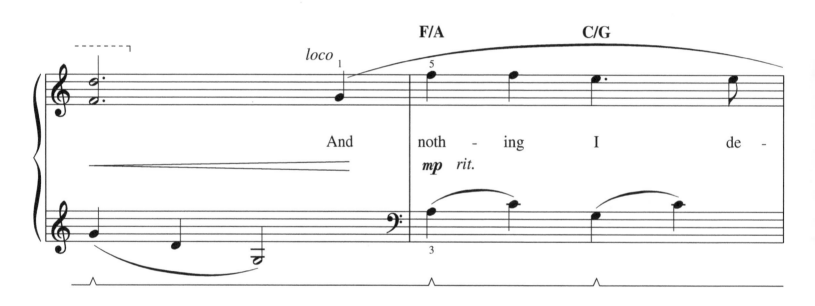

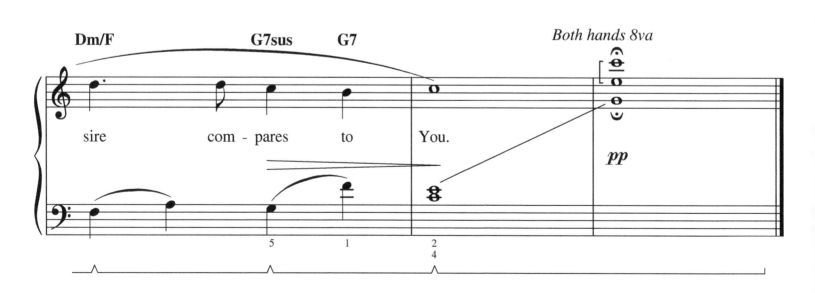

PEOPLE NEED THE LORD

Words and Music by PHILL McHUGH
and GREG NELSON

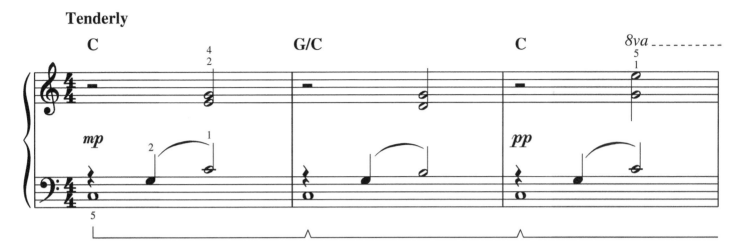

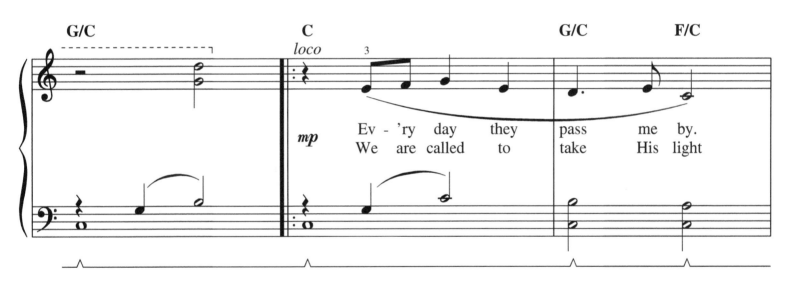

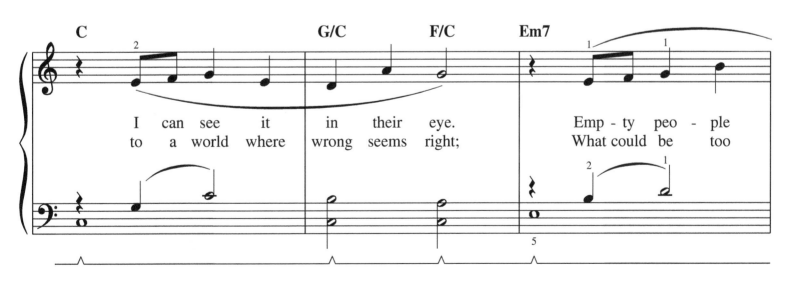

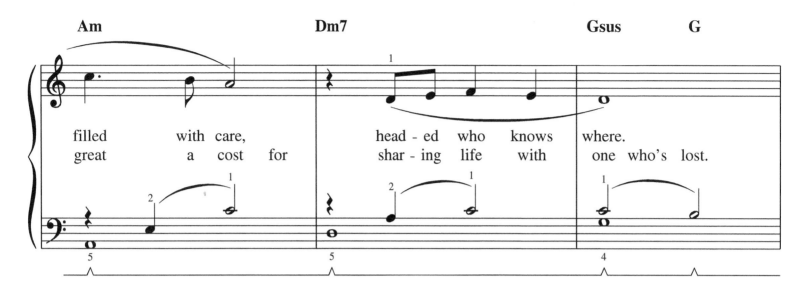

filled with care, / great a cost for
head - ed who knows where. / shar - ing life with one who's lost.

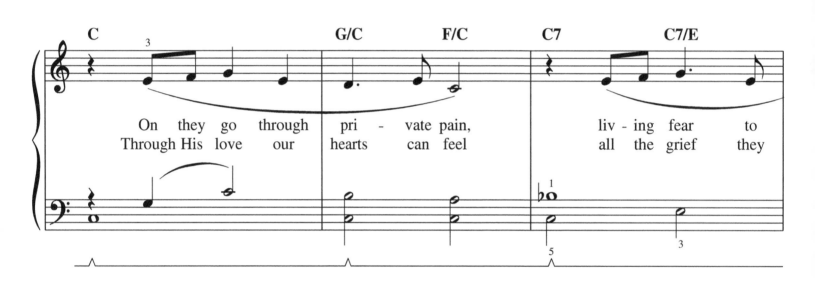

On they go through pri - vate pain, / Through His love our hearts can feel
liv - ing fear to / all the grief they

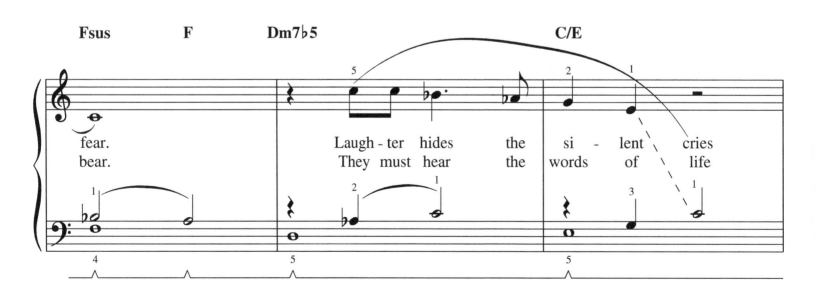

fear. / bear.
Laugh - ter hides the si - lent cries / They must hear the words of life

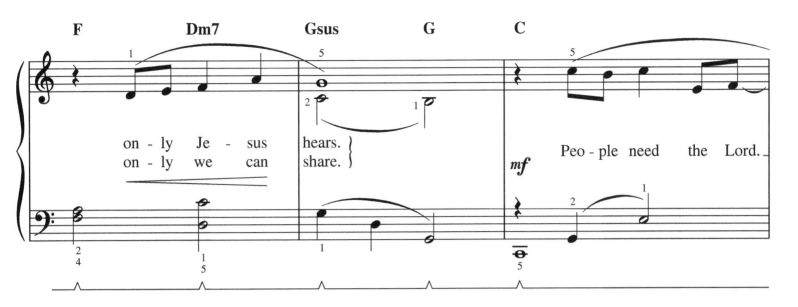

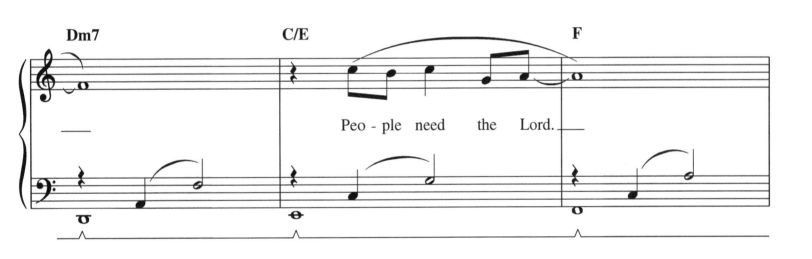

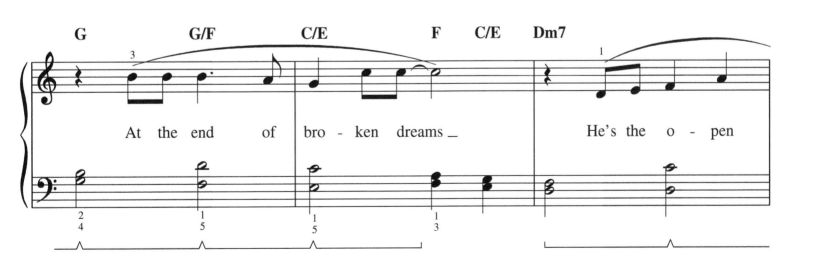

O HOW HE LOVES YOU AND ME

Words and Music by
KURT KAISER

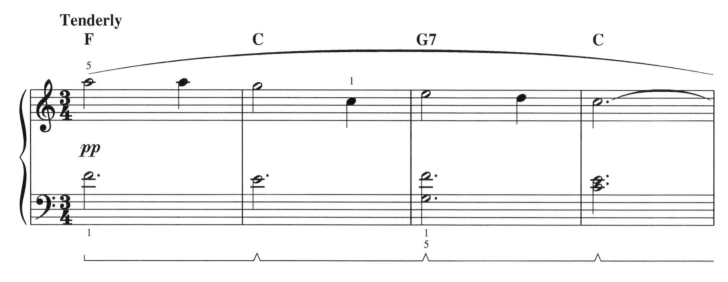

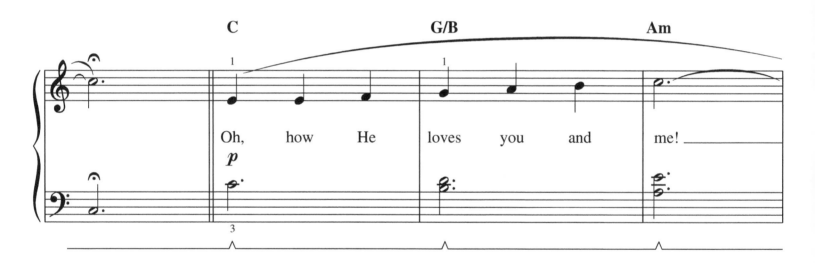

Oh, how He loves you and me!

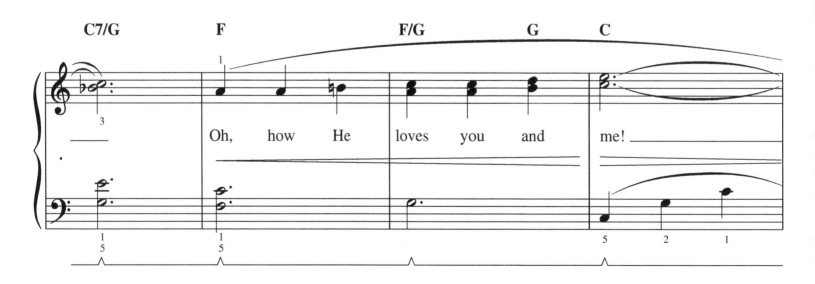

Oh, how He loves you and me!

He gave His life, what __ more could He

pp cresc.

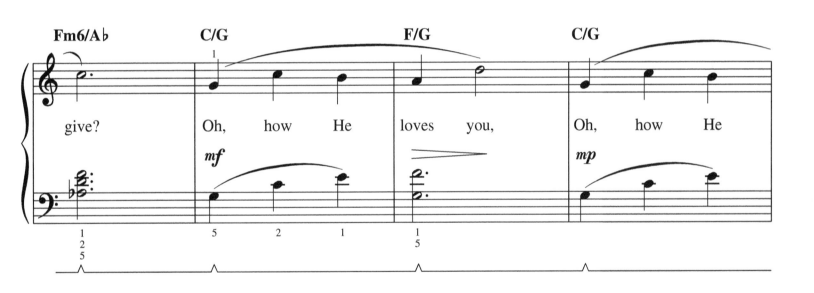

Fm6/A♭   C/G   F/G   C/G

give? Oh, how He loves you, Oh, how He

mf

mp

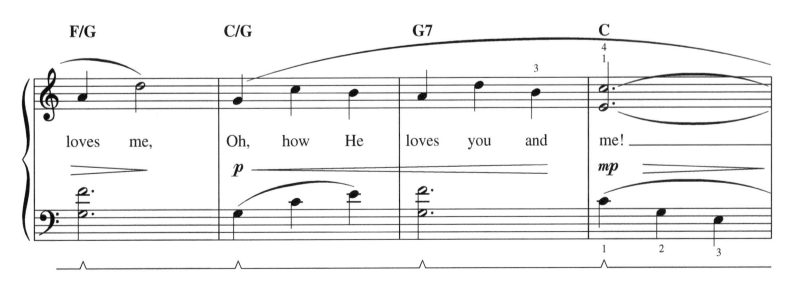

F/G   C/G   G7   C

loves me, Oh, how He loves you and me! __

p

mp

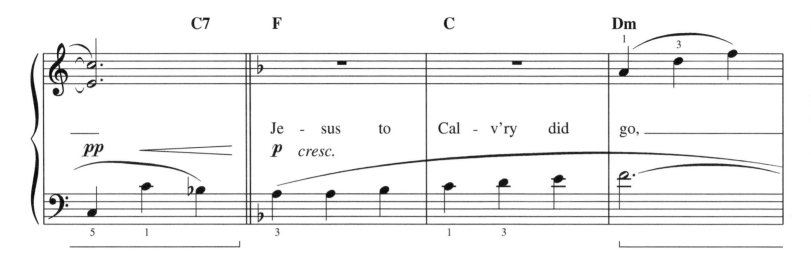

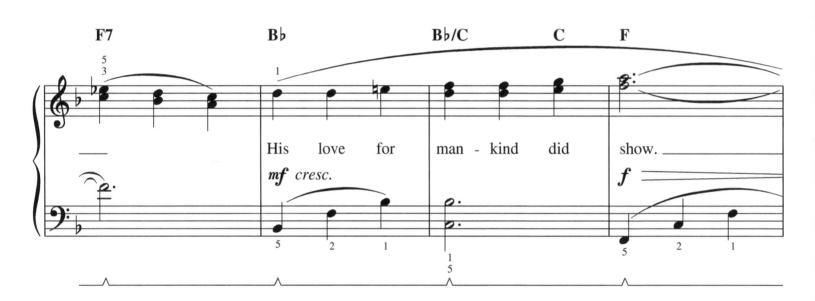

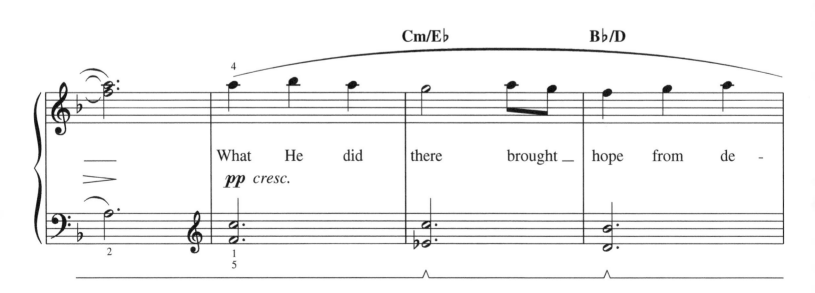

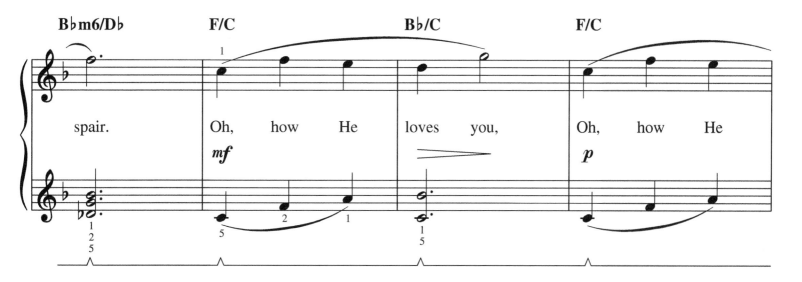

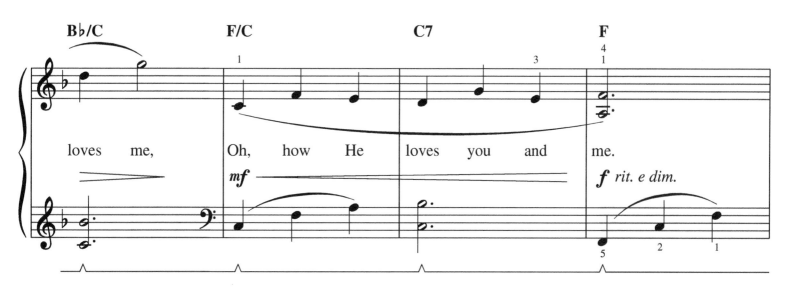

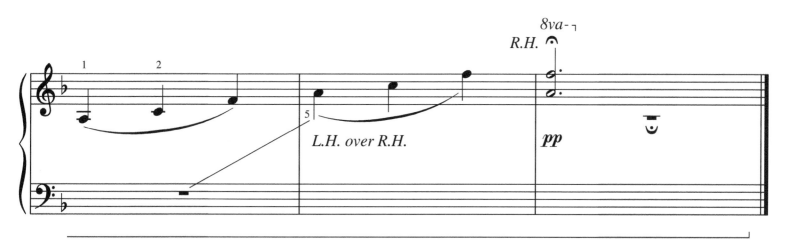

OH LORD, YOU'RE BEAUTIFUL

Words and Music by
KEITH GREEN

Prayerfully, like a choir

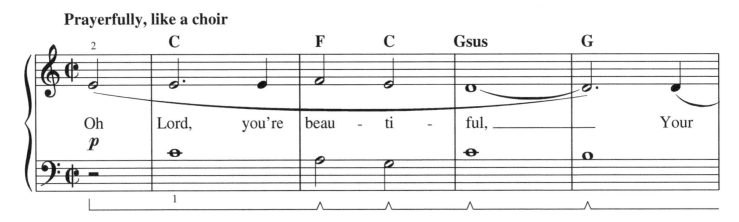

Oh Lord, you're beau - ti - ful, ___ Your

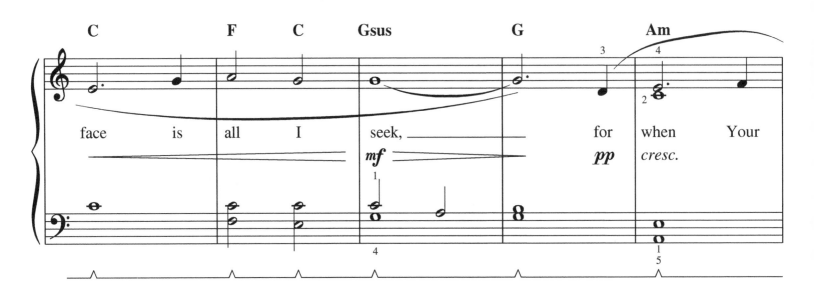

face is all I seek, ___ for when Your

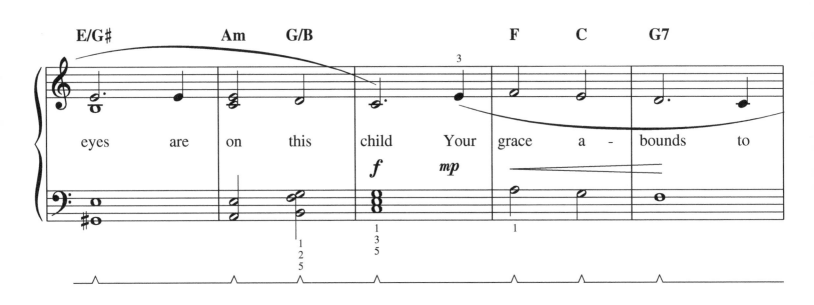

eyes are on this child Your grace a - bounds to

SEEK YE FIRST

Words and Music by
KAREN LAFFERTY

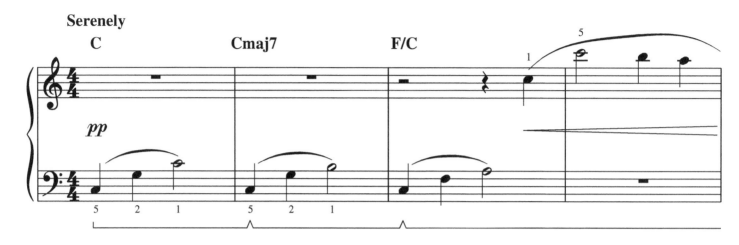

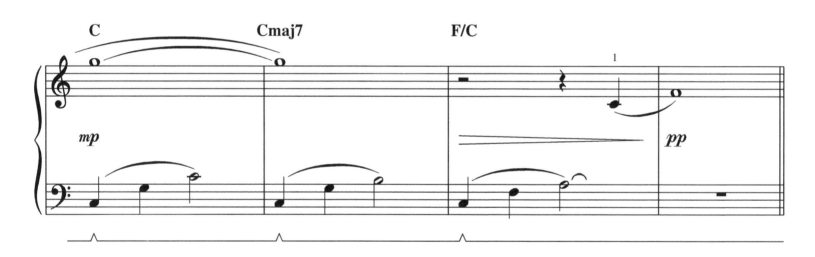

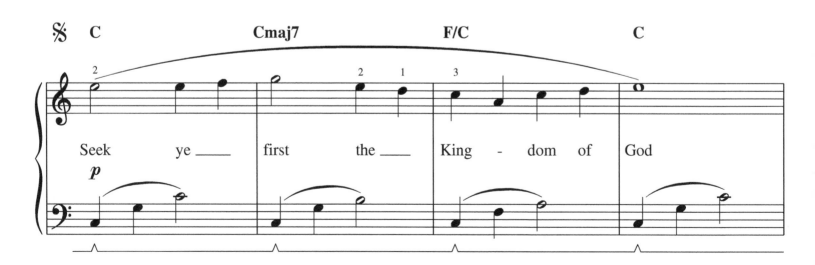

Seek ye ___ first the ___ King - dom of God

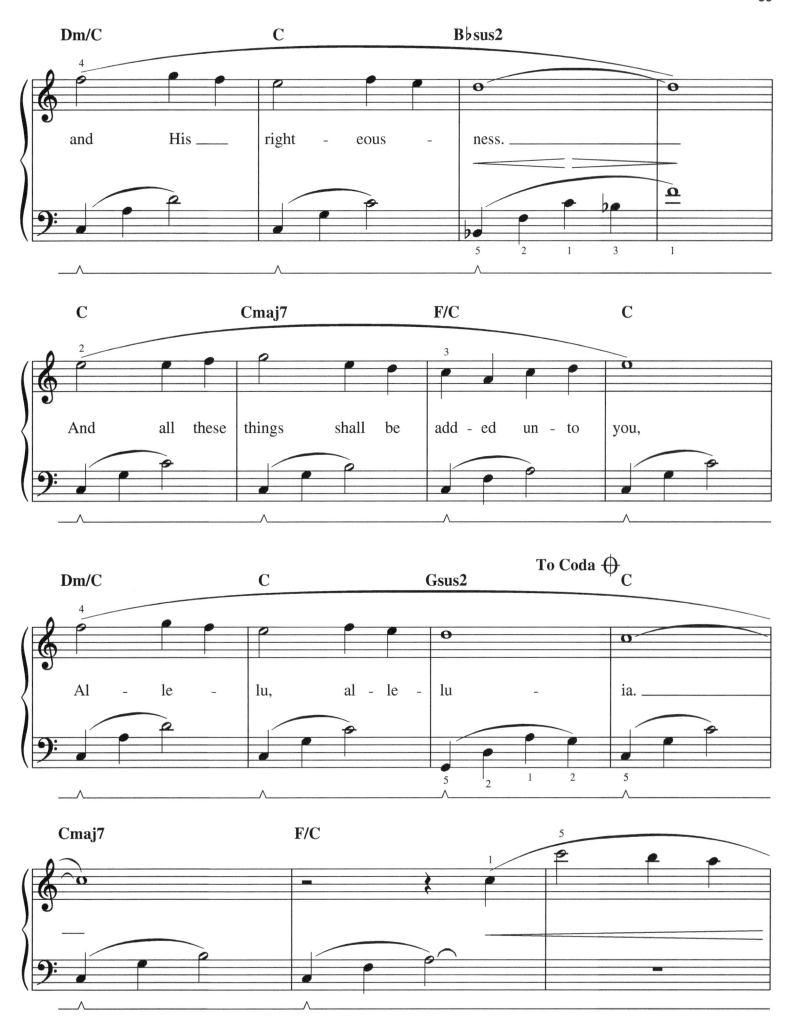

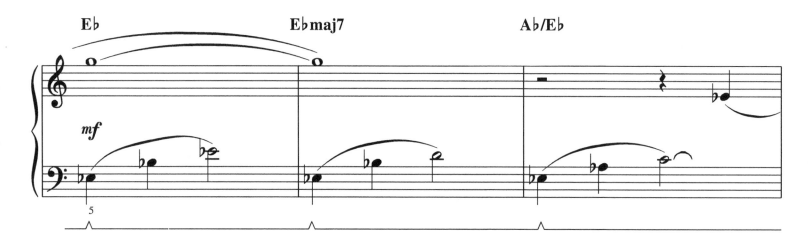

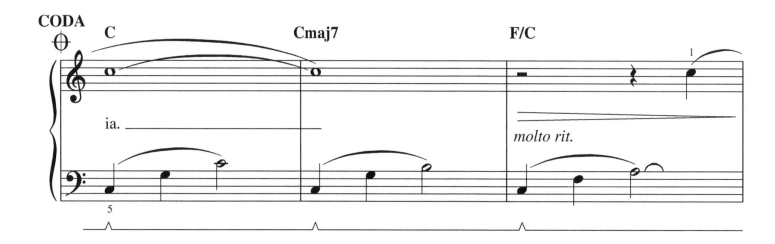

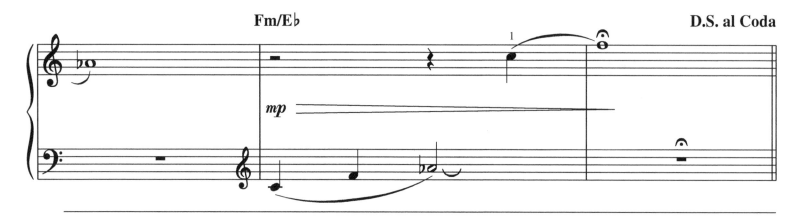

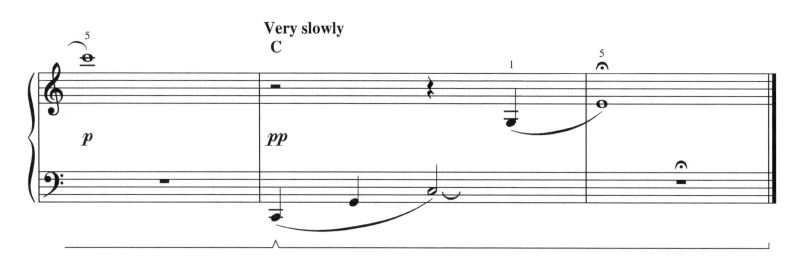

THERE IS A REDEEMER

Words and Music by
MELODY GREEN

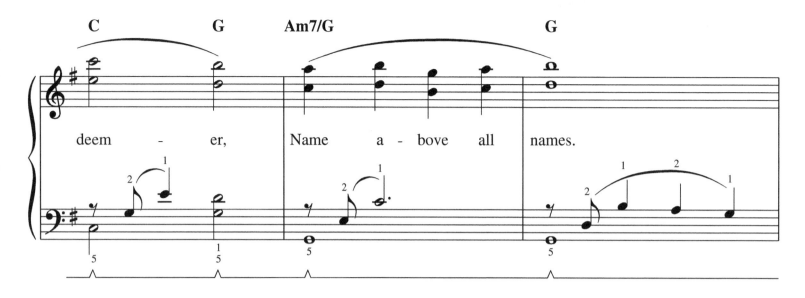

deem - er, Name a - bove all names.

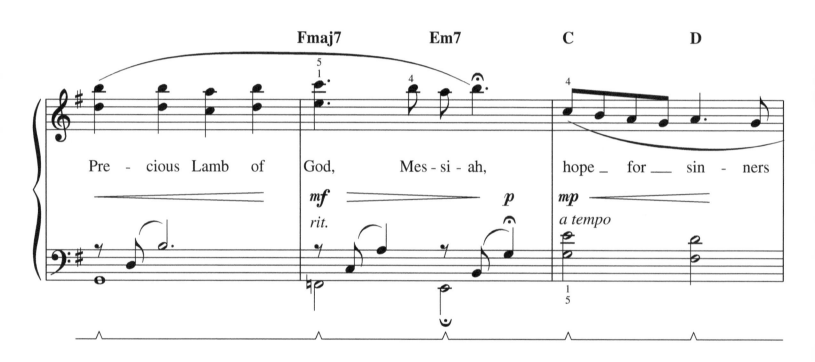

Pre - cious Lamb of God, Mes - si - ah, hope _ for _ sin - ners

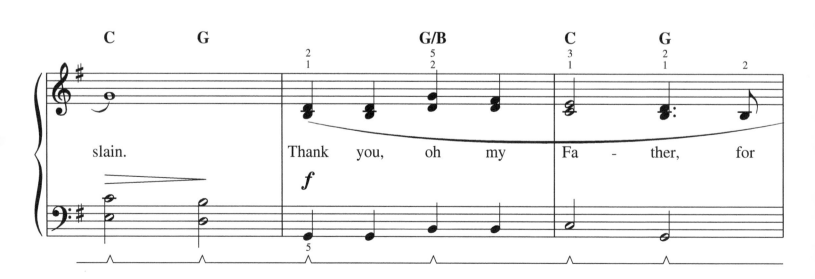

slain. Thank you, oh my Fa - ther, for

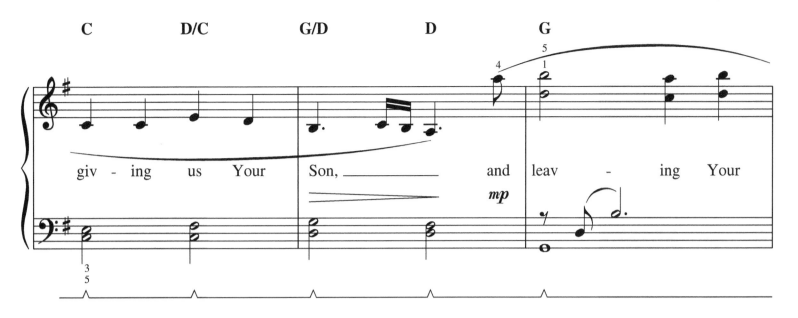

giv - ing us Your Son, _____ and leav - ing Your

mp

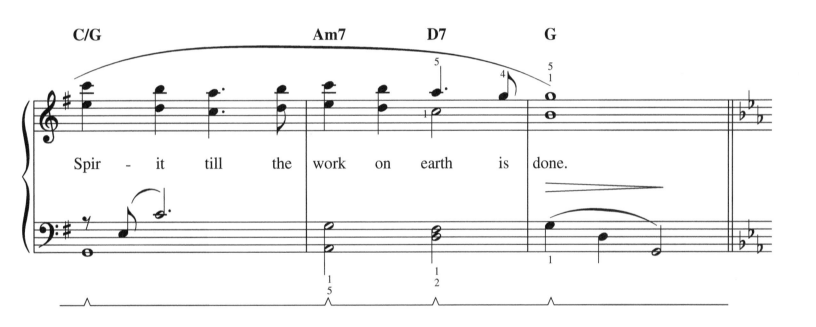

Spir - it till the work on earth is done.

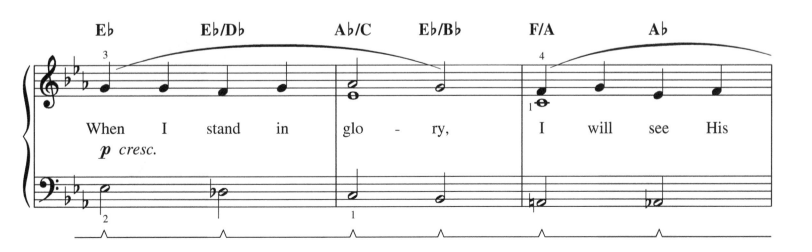

When I stand in glo - ry, I will see His

p cresc.

face, And there I'll serve my King for - ev - er

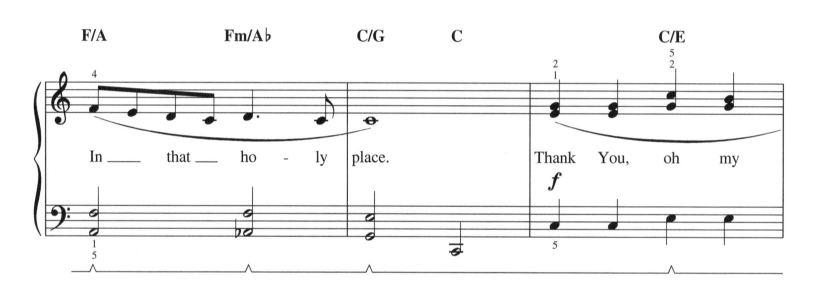

In ___ that ___ ho - ly place. Thank You, oh my

Fa - ther, for giv - ing us Your Son, ___ and

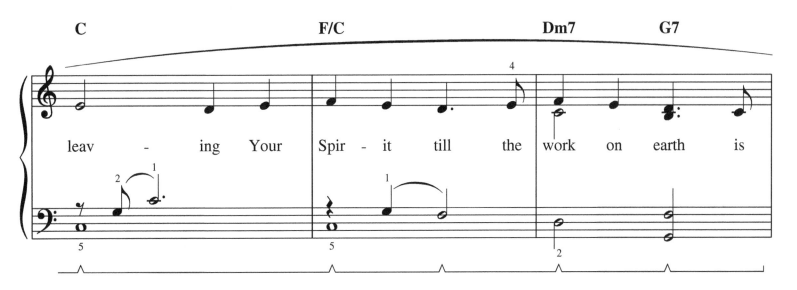

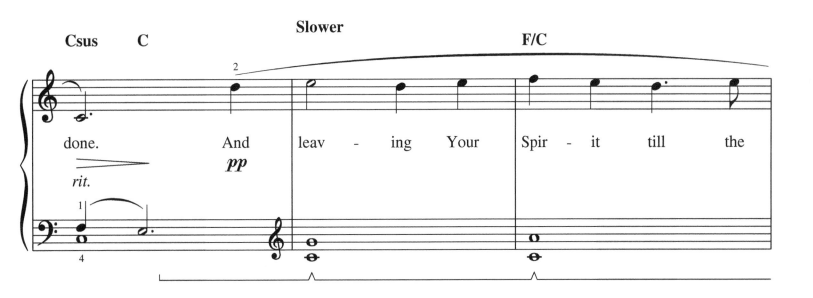

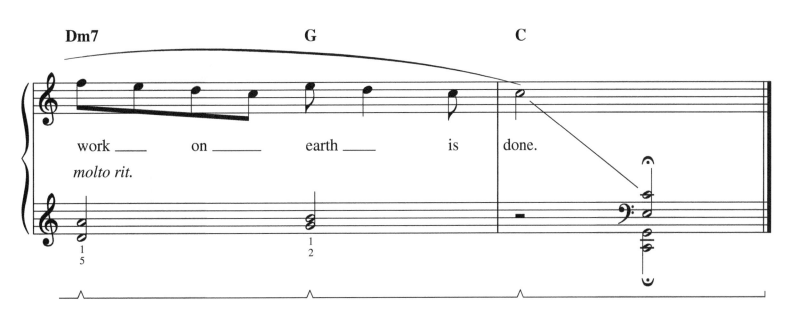

A SHIELD ABOUT ME

Words and Music by DONN THOMAS
and CHARLES WILLIAMS

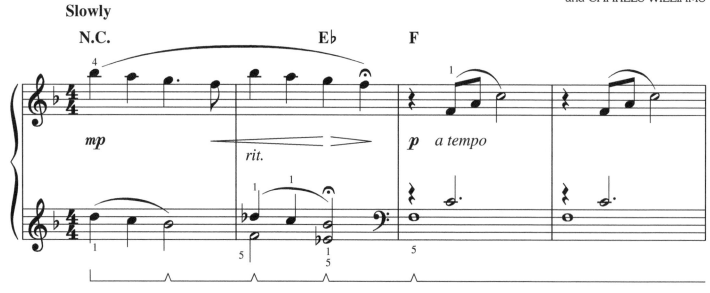

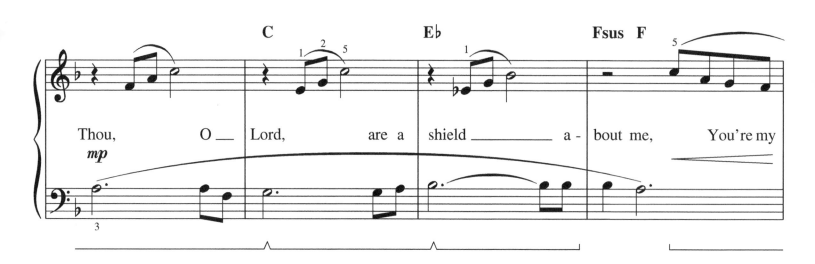

Thou, O Lord, are a shield about me, You're my

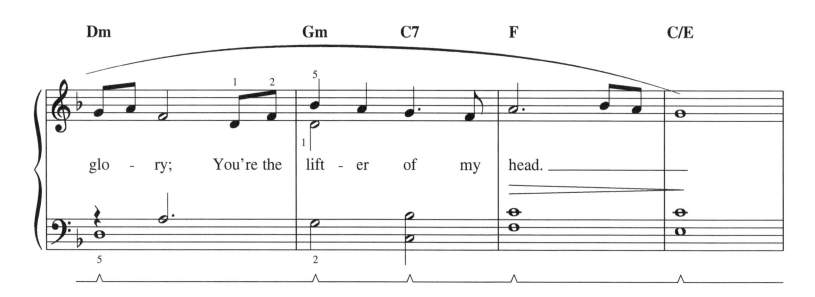

glo-ry; You're the lift-er of my head.

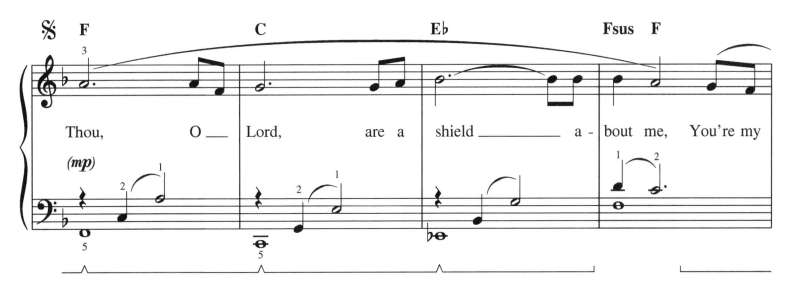

Thou, O __ Lord, are a shield _____ a - bout me, You're my

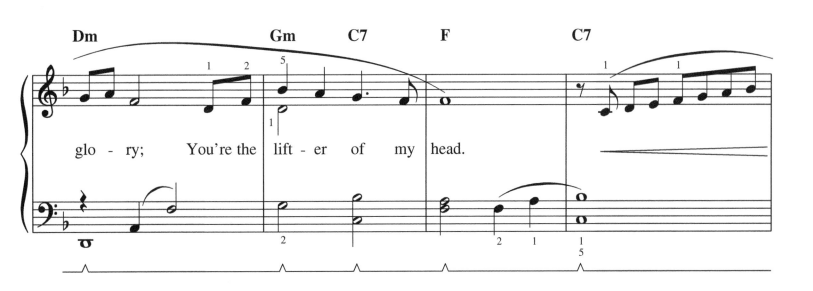

glo - ry; You're the lift - er of my head.

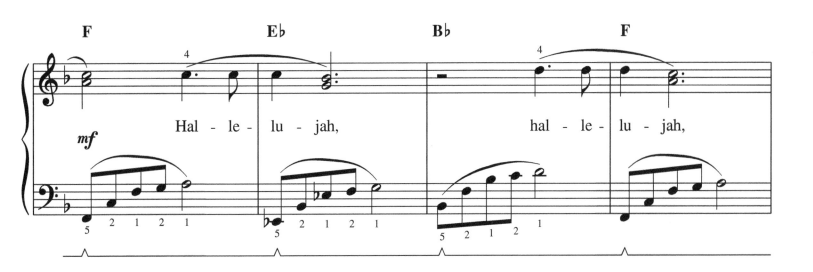

Hal - le - lu - jah, hal - le - lu - jah,

To Coda ⊕

hal - le - lu - jah,   You're the lift - er of my

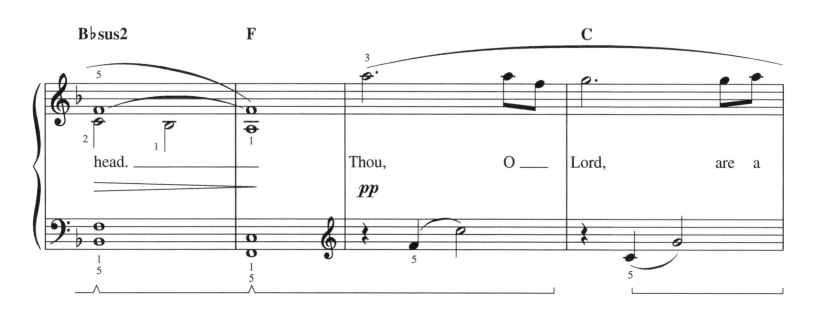

head. ____ Thou,   O ____ Lord,   are a

pp

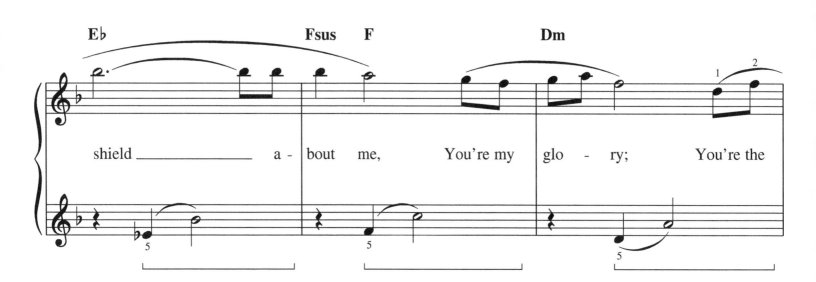

shield _____ a - bout me,   You're my glo - ry;   You're the

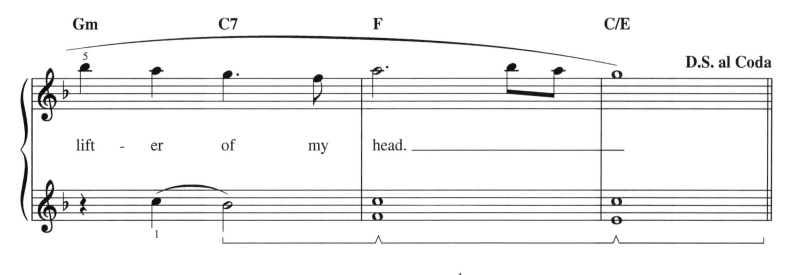

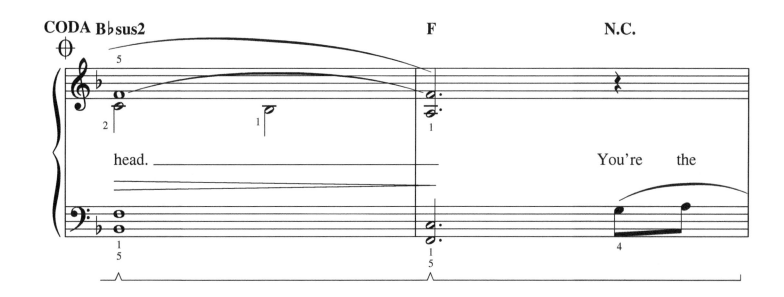

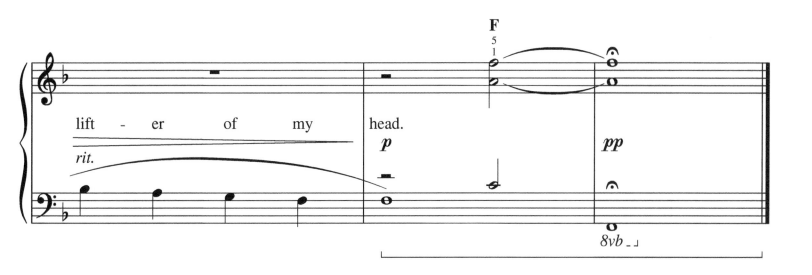

SHINE, JESUS, SHINE

Words and Music by
GRAHAM KENDRICK

With spirit

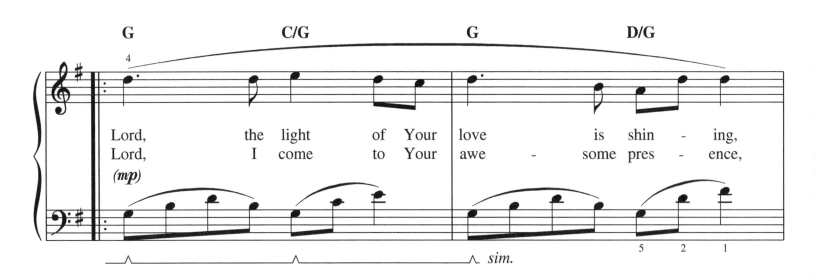

Lord, the light of Your love is shin - ing,
Lord, I come to Your awe - some pres - ence,

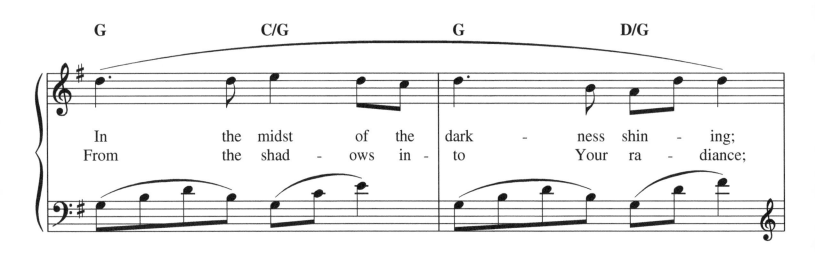

In the midst of the dark - ness shin - ing;
From the shad - ows in - to Your ra - diance;

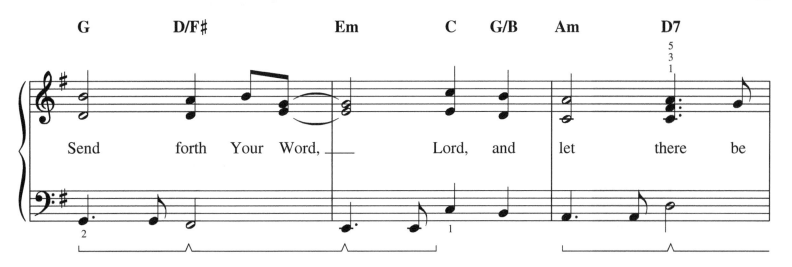

Send   forth   Your Word, ___   Lord,   and   let   there   be

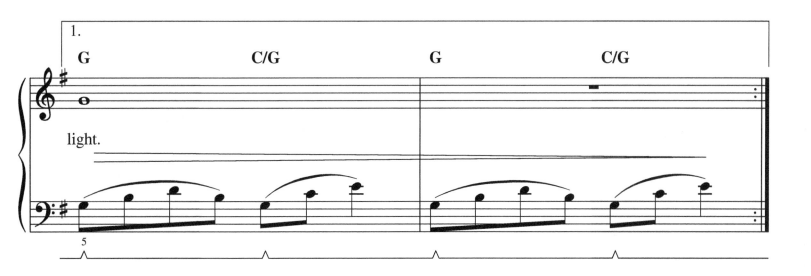

1.

light.

2.

light.   Lord,   and   let   there   be   light.

molto rit.

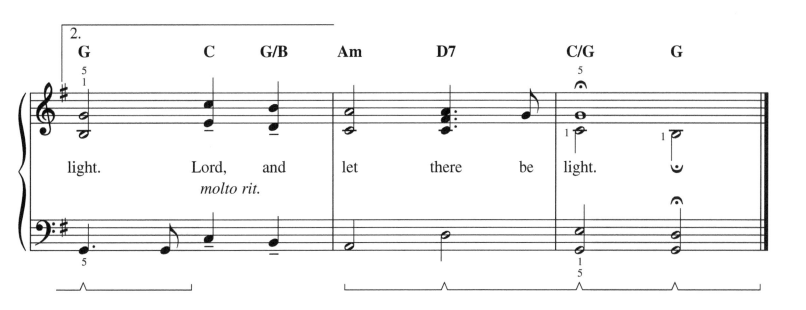

SHOUT TO THE LORD

Words and Music by
DARLENE ZSCHECH

Slowly and expressively

My Je - sus, my Sav - ior; Lord, there is none _ like You. All of my days _ I want to praise _ the won-der of Your might - y love.

75

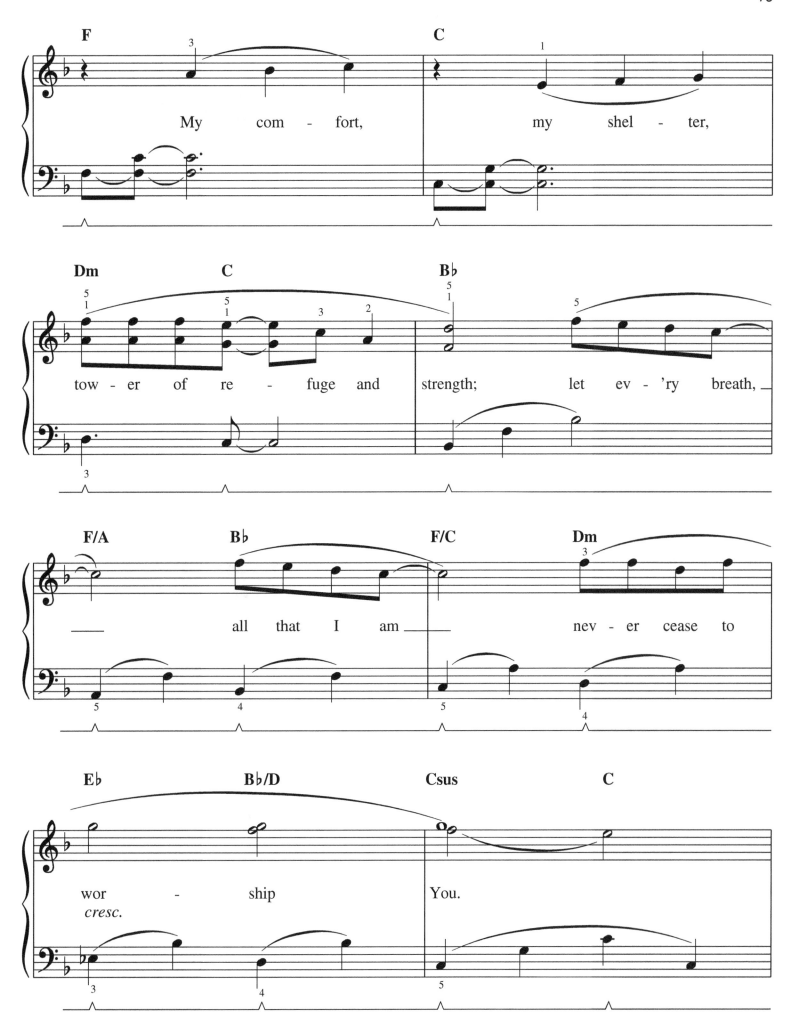

THY WORD

Words and Music by MICHAEL W. SMITH
and AMY GRANT

Moderately, expressively

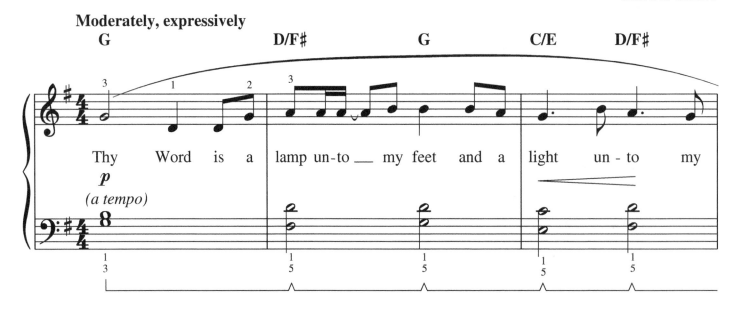

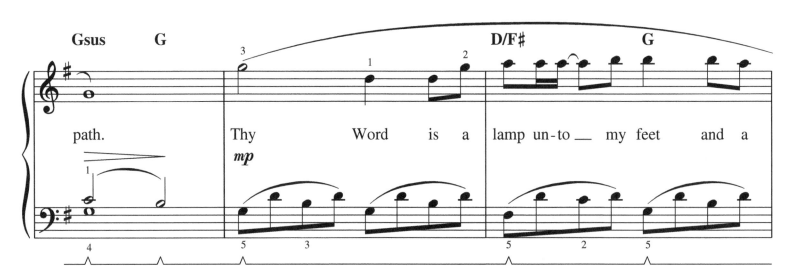

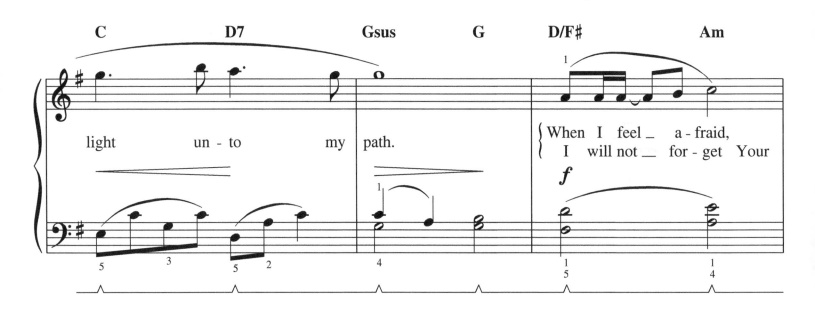

Thy Word is a lamp un-to __ my feet and a light un-to my path.

Thy Word is a lamp un-to __ my feet and a light un-to my path.

When I feel __ a-fraid, I will not __ for-get Your

think I've lost — my way, still You're there right be - side me.
love for me — and yet my heart for - ev - er is won - d'ring.

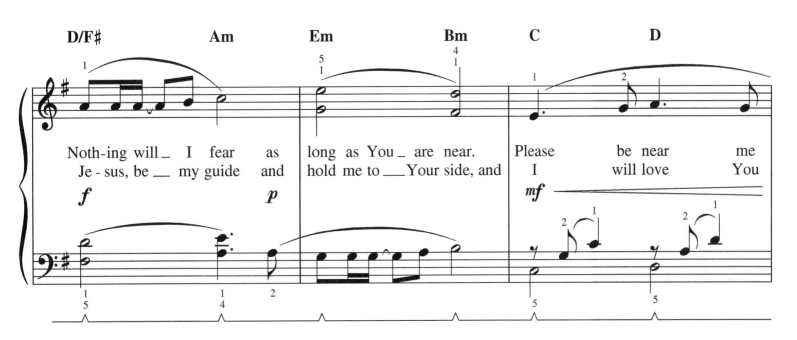

Noth-ing will — I fear as long as You — are near. Please be near me
Je - sus, be — my guide and hold me to — Your side, and I will love You

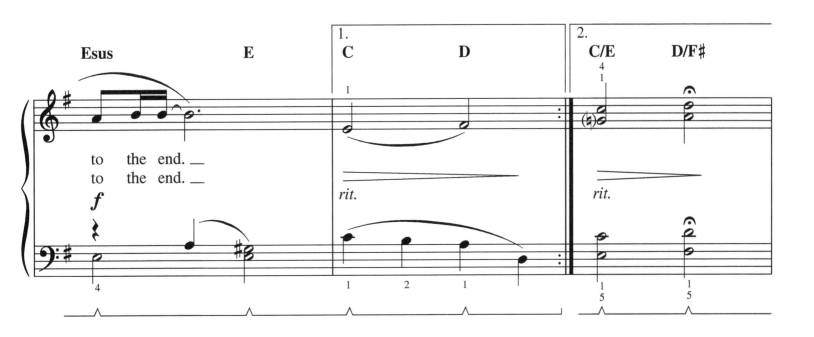

to the end. —
to the end. —

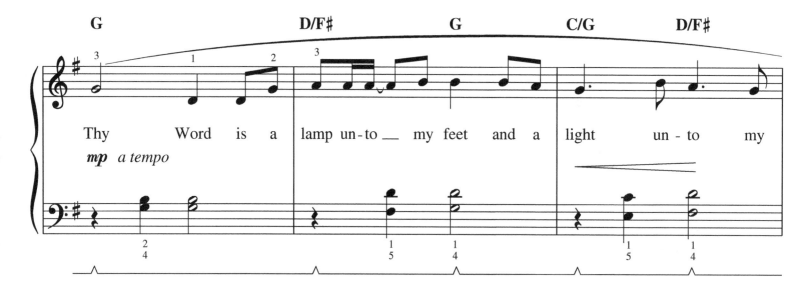

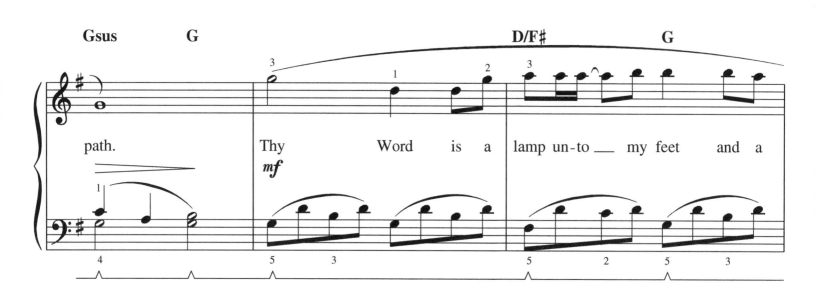

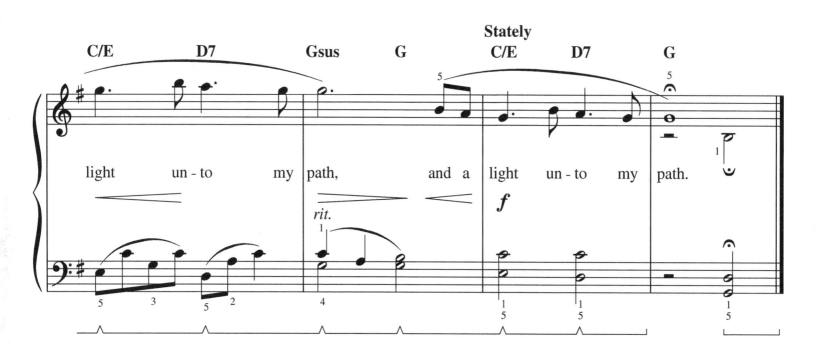